Information System Implementations: Using a Leadership Quality Matrix for Success

Information System Implementations: Using a Leadership Quality Matrix for Success

System Implementations, Gain Significant Momentum,
An Insiders Guide to What you need to know

Andries J Jacobs

AuthorHouse™
1663 Liberty Drive
Bloomington, IN 47403
www.authorhouse.com
Phone: 1-800-839-8640

© 2012 by Andries J Jacobs. All rights reserved.

No part of this book may be reproduced, stored in a retrieval system, or transmitted by any means without the written permission of the author.

First published by AuthorHouse   01/21/2012

ISBN: 978-1-4685-4115-1 (sc)
ISBN: 978-1-4685-4114-4 (hc)
ISBN: 978-1-4685-4113-7 (ebk)

Library of Congress Control Number: 2012900442

Printed in the United States of America

Any people depicted in stock imagery provided by Thinkstock are models, and such images are being used for illustrative purposes only.
Certain stock imagery © Thinkstock.

This book is printed on acid-free paper.

Because of the dynamic nature of the Internet, any web addresses or links contained in this book may have changed since publication and may no longer be valid. The views expressed in this work are solely those of the author and do not necessarily reflect the views of the publisher, and the publisher hereby disclaims any responsibility for them.

Contents

Preface ix
Acknowledgments xiii
Introduction xv

Section One
Getting Ready for the Trip

Chapter One   Background to the Leadership Quality Matrix 3
Chapter Two   Stakeholders 13
     Topic Introduction 13
         Organizational Team 13
         Project Team 17
     From a Modified Leader's Pen 20
Chapter Three   Implementation Process 24
     Topic Introduction 24
     From a Modified Leader's Pen 27

Section Two
The Trip

Chapter Four   Project Management 33
     Topic Introduction 33
     From a Modified Leader's Pen 34
         System-Implementation Manager 35
         Team Leaders 36
         Executive Sponsor 37
         All Project Team Members 38
     Assessing Your Project-Management Quotient 38
         System-Implementation Manager 38
         Team Leaders 39

  Executive Sponsor 40
  All Project Team Members 40
Chapter Five Process Standardization 41
 Topic Introduction 41
 From a Modified Leader's Pen 42
  Business-Process Owner 42
  Business-Functional Experts 43
  Functional and Technical Consultants 44
  Key Users 44
 Assessing Your Project-Management Quotient 45
  Business-Process Owner 45
  Business-Functional Experts 45
  Functional and Technical Consultants
  Key Users 46
Chapter Six Project Transition 47
 Topic Introduction 47
 From a Modified Leader's Pen 48
  Senior Management 48
  Business-Process Owner 49
  End Users 49
  System-Implementation Manager 50
  Functional and Technical Consultants 50
  Key Users 51
 Assessing Your Project-Management Quotient 51
  Senior Management 52
  Business-Process Owner 52
  End Users 52
  System-Implementation Manager 52
  Functional and Technical Consultants 53
  Key Users 53
Chapter Seven Benefit Realization 54
 Topic Introduction 54
 From a Modified Leader's Pen 55
  Business Management 55
  Business-Functional Experts 56
  Executive Sponsor 56
  Key and End Users 57
 Assessing Your Project-Management Quotient 57

Business Management 57
Executive Sponsor 58
Key and End Users 58
Chapter Eight   Troubleshooting 60
Topic Introduction 60
From a Modified Leader's Pen 61
End Users 62
Key Users 62
Service and Support Teams 63
Assessing Your Project-Management Quotient 63
Business-Functional Experts 63
End Users 64
Key Users 64
Service and Support Teams 64

Section Three
Diagnostic Instruments

Chapter Nine   Selection of Diagnostic Instruments 69
Topic Introduction 69
Project Management 70
Process Standardization 70
Transition 70
Business Realization 70
Troubleshooting 70
Diagnostic Instruments 71
Personality Grid 71
Group-Development Process 72
Decision-Authority Leadership Model 73
Superior-Subordinate Power-Relationship Model 75
Supportive vs. Directive Behavior Leadership Model 76
Leadership vs. Management Matrix 77
Strategic Side vs. Personal Sides of Leadership Model 78
From a Modified Leader's Pen 79
Personality Grid 79
Group-Development Process 80
Decision-Authority Leadership Model 80
Superior-Subordinate Power-Relationship Model 80

      Supportive vs. Directive Behavior Leadership Model 80
      Leadership vs. Management Matrix 81
      Strategic Side vs. Personal Sides of Leadership Model 81
   Assessing Your Project-Management Quotient 81
Conclusion... 85
   Topic Introduction 85
   From a Modified Leader's Pen 86
Appendix A: A Step-by-Step Approach 87
Appendix B: Leadership Quality Matrix 89
Appendix C: Diagnostic Instruments 95
References 97
Recommended Reading... 99
Index... 101

About the Author 103

Preface

Welcome to *Information System Implementations: Using a Leadership Quality Matrix for Success*. Take a couple of hours, sit back, relax, and gain intellectual capital for your knowledge workers, geared toward providing significant momentum to your system implementations and based on my twenty-four years of software-development, system-management, and system-implementation experience, from both a consulting and an operational perspective.

I must begin by emphasizing that this book and its insights are based on my personal experience and mine only. Furthermore, this book is not intended to be an exhaustive list of facts; it includes only those that deserve our immediate attention. I recognize that some people will not agree with what I have written, and that's okay. I also know that some people might disagree with the concepts presented here. Although my experience may not be the same as yours, I feel these concepts will be useful to you.

In *Information System Implementations: Using a Leadership Quality Matrix for Success*, I have tried to create an easy-to-follow, all-you-need-to-know road map that will not only help the organization and system-implementation team members understand the theory behind leadership and leadership qualities, but also show, from the perspective of a "modified leader," how to apply these traits to their particular system-implementation projects. Let me explain what I mean by "modified leader."

Over the last fourteen years, my strong interest in the topic of leadership and my awareness that success is hard to come by prompted me to read about and study the topic of leadership, whether in autobiographies or textbooks. One of my hallmarks is my willingness to implement—within the organizations where I have led system operations or have implemented systems—the very best leadership ideas out there, regardless of where they originate. Those of you who are practicing leadership and teaching it to your followers (hopefully most of you, as this is the way that your system implementation will gain significant momentum) will understand the way that exceptional and well-published authors like John Maxwell, Peter Urs Bender, Stephen Covey, Manfred Kets de Vries, Peter Koestenbaum, Oren Harari, Larry Julian, and Colin Powell have impacted my life and stimulated the modified leadership passion in me.

"Modified leader" is a term that will be used in this book to reflect the opinions of the author. The term "modified leader" is an indication that the author acknowledges his leadership thinking and leadership style have changed based on a thorough understanding of the differences between management and leadership and a thorough understanding of what leadership qualities are and how prominent business individuals lead by example. The modified leader comments are reflective of the leadership style the author has adopted and practiced with the insights gained from exceptional and well-published authors and applied experience as an information system-implementation leader.

People always ask me why I wanted to write this book, and I can highlight two notable incidents or inspirations that provided the spark.

The first was about five years ago, when I had taken and boiled down my notes into little gems and presented them at Sapphire 2003 (an annual SAP user conference) in Orlando, Florida, in a presentation called "Leadership Requirements for Rapid Implementation of a Global SAP solution." In 2005, I delivered the same presentation at the PMI (a professional organization for the project management profession), Ontario chapter in Toronto. Attendees enjoyed it and encouraged me to do something with the material other than presenting it to selected audiences.

The second inspiration was all the bad publicity over the last couple of decades around company-wide business-system implementations. Consider, for example, the following facts:

- Tata Consulting in 2007 reported that 49 percent of IT projects reported overruns, 41 percent failed to deliver expected business value, and 33 percent failed to perform up to expectations (Galorath, June 7, 2008).
- Analyst firm Gartner estimates that 55 to 75 percent of all ERP (Enterprise Resource Planning) projects fail to meet their objectives (http://erp.asia/erp-failures.asp).
- A report from the European Services Strategy Unity, an independent watchdog agency, found that 57 percent of IT-related contracts experienced overruns, 33 percent of contracts experienced major delays, and 30 percent of contracts were cancelled (Michael Krigsman, January 10, 2008).
- A report by Panorama Consulting on small business ERP projects (projects valued at a few millions of dollars) found that 61.1 percent of projects take longer than expected, 74.1 percent of projects exceeded costs, and 48 percent of projects realized less than 50 percent benefits (Michael Krigsman, March 1, 2011).

The list goes on and on. As a specialist in information systems and project management, I view it as my responsibility to act as a change agent, addressing the perception that leadership is a management function only. This is what schools are teaching us. My success to date stems from the fact that, as a modified leader, I always try to speak to the collective imagination of my team and focus on the personality variables rather than environmental constraints. In my selection of and dealing with team members, my focus is always on their personality and behavior.

I hope and believe that whether you run a small or large system-implementation project or are a team member on a system implementation, you will benefit from applying the content of this book the way I have. Once the organization and project-team members grasp the concept, they will respond with urgency to become key players and gain significant momentum for their system implementation.

Acknowledgments

Dear Lord, almost four years ago, I wrote the first words of this book. Thank you for somehow guiding me through a process completely foreign to me. I have come to understand how You bless me through others.

I would like to thank the group of people who have helped me the most to achieve clarity in the topic of *Information System Implementations: Using a Leadership Quality Matrix for Success.*

To my incredible parents, Frans and Martha—words cannot express how much I love you both. I am truly grateful for your never-ending love and encouragement. Your belief in my abilities and your constant cheering through the good as well as the challenging times have allowed me to keep pushing forward.

My wife, Anna, has already received her share of accolades in some of my prior studies, but in this case, she outdid herself. During the time I wrote this book, we did not spend a lot of time together. If I wasn't on international assignments, I was in my office hunched over a laptop surrounded by a mound of manuscripts. Anna hung in there, took care of the home and the family, and provided me with a foundation of love and support that was essential for my ability to complete this mission.

My two wonderful daughters, Alicia and Mariska—thank you for hanging in there while I was away on international assignments. Thank you for being the good students you have been. I am proud of you; you are beautiful and wonderful. Good luck with your future professional careers.

To my brother, Michiel—congratulations on all your successes. Most importantly, thank you for being such an amazing brother and such a great friend.

To my brother's family and my wife's family—thank you for your support and encouragement over the years.

To my business partner, Timothy Perley-Robertson—thank you for taking care of the business while I was out of the office working on other assignments and this book.

Thanks to all my colleagues, team members, and friends in Brazil, Canada, Kazakhstan, Russia, South Africa, and the United Kingdom who have worked on projects with me. I learned from all of you and built up the experience to write this book.

Thank you all. There is no way in the world that I could pull this off without you.

As I started, I want to end by expressing how grateful I am to God. Romans 12:3–8 confirms that the leadership quality matrix has been ours since the earliest days:

> Do not think of yourself more highly than you ought, but rather think of yourself with sober judgment, in accordance with the measure of faith God has given you. Just as each of us has one body with many members, and these members do not all have the same function, so in Christ we who are many form one body, and each member belongs to all the others. We have different gifts, according to the grace given us. If a man's gift is prophesying, let him use it in proportion to his faith. If it is serving, let him serve; if it is teaching, let him teach; if it is encouraging, let him encourage; if it is contributing to the needs of others, let him give generously; if it is leadership, let him govern diligently; if it is showing mercy, let him do it cheerfully. (Hayford, Middlebrook, and Matsdorf, 1991:1508–1509)

Introduction

Primarily, this book provides insight into a leadership quality matrix that can be applied during information system implementations. The leadership quality matrix provides, with regard to information system-implementation projects, a three-dimensional relationship between roles and responsibilities required to support the implementation process, the various implementation process focus areas, and leadership qualities required to support the implementation process. The leadership quality matrix is built up with a thorough understanding of the various stakeholders involved, the applicable implementation process focus areas, and leadership models to determine if potential team members have the required leadership qualities.

The leadership quality matrix is a guideline to recruitment specialists during the identification and selection of potential team members, system integrators during the placement and guidance of team members, and information system users.

Each chapter introduces a specific topic of relevance, explains it, and shows how it can be applied to other company system implementations. To achieve this and help you, the reader, think like a modified leader, each chapter includes the following:

Topic Introduction

Each chapter begins with an introduction that provides insight into the particular topic addressed in the chapter. This outline is based on thoughts and viewpoints of well-respected and published leaders as outlined in the reference section of this book.

From a Modified Leader's Pen

Right after the introduction, I offer my own views and direction based on twenty-four years of experience and accomplishments in software development, system management, and project management, from both a consulting and an operational perspective.

Assessing Your Project-Management Quotient

Most of the chapters or topics end with a brief assessment exercise. The intent is to put organization and project-team members through the test to ascertain whether the project employs the practice of the relevant leadership quality topic.

In chapter one of this book I describe five system implementations that formed the basis for the notes that I boiled down as little gems and presented to appreciative audiences in Orlando and Toronto. Take a look at them and see if your system-implementation experiences are similar.

An analysis of these five project initiatives over the past fourteen years allowed me to formulate the leadership quality matrix for the various system-implementation roles and responsibilities. It also formed the foundation for the definition of critical success factors, roles, responsibilities, and leadership qualities.

Section One

Getting Ready for the Trip

Chapter One

Background to the Leadership Quality Matrix

In this chapter, I'll offer you a synopsis of the five most challenging system implementations in which I have participated to provide an understanding of not only my system-implementation experience and the challenges my various teams and I had to deal with, but also my insights into the system-implementation environments that have molded the modified leader in me and contributed to the development of the leadership quality matrix.

From a Modified Leader's Pen

Project 1. In May 1996, as director of marketing administration, I had just researched and developed for the fertilizer industry in South Africa a price-decision, support-system, functional-user specification, and was then assigned the task of client system-implementation lead for the northern region to lead a SAP R/3 version 4.0 h system implementation. The team delivered the SAP R/3 version 4.0 h implementation slightly outside the budget of US$3 million and the scheduled implementation period of twelve months. The configuration and implementation effort included the FI/CO (finance and corporate controlling), SD/MM (sales and materials management), PP (production planning), AM (asset management), and HR (human resources) modules. The infrastructure-technology platform, which at the time was leading-edge, consisted of HP hardware, Oracle database, and Unix operating system. The technical team implemented a three-tier development landscape.

The primary goal was to migrate from a corporate business system developed in-house—including finance, costing, and sales—to an integrated, process-driven enterprise resource planning (ERP) system. The results were remarkable: we reduced onetime plant-maintenance inventory by 30 percent, stock levels on a month-by-month basis by 15 percent, distribution costs by 10 percent, customer complaints by 2 percent, and administration cost by 1 percent.

As Winston Churchill once said, "I was strengthened by the critics' comments." Throughout the implementation, there was no lack of criticism, which in the end contributed to the molding of the modified leader in me and the understanding that leadership is a team effort rather than a management-only issue.

The team experienced a wide range of challenges related to people, process, and technology, including:

- Building an information-technology (IT) and systems team using the regional talent pool
- Dealing with poor IT infrastructure between regional headquarters and distribution and sales offices
- Transforming from a mainframe to a client-server environment
- Working with management's ability to design software for solution-supported business processes
- Getting regional alignment within the broader organization
- Developing processes and procedures that fit the real-time client-server environment
- Getting employees computer-literate enough to be trained in the new transaction-based client-server environment
- Motivating employees to execute transactions according to the flow and order of the business process
- Operating the business as an integrated unit (production, sales, procurement, maintenance, and finance)
- Restructuring administrative departments
- Avoiding putting the business at risk
- Getting system-output acceptance

Project 2. In August 2001, as information-system consultant and part of a high-performance management team, I performed a forward-looking assessment for the largest city in Canada of the value-for-money of the process-control-system and IT components of the program-integration and coordination-services contract. When a carpool friend and colleague was suddenly sidelined by a medical condition, I also took the responsibility to lead the Lawson Enterprise Resource Planning conference-room pilot project.

I led the team with a focus on implementing a resource-related software solution, including the design of the selection criteria, software selection process, vendor qualification, and project recommendation and approval processes. The outcome was the rejection of the proposed system and selection of SAP R/3 version 4.6 d as the preferred ERP business system.

The centralized resource-related SAP R/3 implementation was for a global engineering-services company with forty-seven offices on all major continents around the world. Major offices were located in Australia, South Africa, the United Kingdom, Canada, the United States, and Chile. The team had an outstanding performance and implemented, within eight months, the FI/CO, SD/MM, PS (project systems), HR, ITS (Internet transaction services), and employee self-service modules. A company strategic direction drove the infrastructure-technology platform, consisting of Microsoft operating system, Compaq hardware, and SQL database. As a team, we developed, implemented, and managed the global operational-support infrastructure, including the help-desk environment. The support team implemented and managed the global training-program and learning-material-development environments. The support team consisted of sixty people, delivering training to three thousand employees globally.

The main focus of the project was to amalgamate three legacy systems (SAP R/3 version 2.2, Oracle, and SUN) and three different company business processes into a single SAP R/3 version 4.6 d system. The US$10 million implementation effort reduced time spent on reconciling and management of time sheets among various countries by 50 percent, invoice time out to customers in Australia from five to three working days, effort of reconciling intercompany accounts by 50 percent, and time spent on data transfer between various systems by 75 percent.

The system implementation challenged the team leadership's capability mainly in terms of environment, people, process, and to a lesser extent technical issues. The key factors derived from this implementation vastly contributed to the understanding of the importance and management of leadership qualities of all team members in reaching successful implementation completion. The team leadership skills and qualities were challenged by:

- The big-bang rollout approach
- The project being managed by me as a company employee, supported by a vendor-assigned system-implementation manager
- The incorporation of three different companies and three different systems into a single centralized system
- A management style and diverse business requirements that resulted in conflicting system requirements
- Differing backgrounds of project-team members from the United States, South Africa, and Australia
- The team's makeup of seven independent consultants, seven internal consultants, and seven business experts
- Business requirements, training, and rollout stretching across multiple time zones, religions, cultures, legislation, and languages

Project 3. In August 2003, as SAP technology manager, I led a team of SAP R/3 professionals supporting global engineering services of SAP R/3 systems in six countries and forty-seven offices around the world. Through leadership-quality development, the team improved the overall end-user satisfaction and system acceptance, reducing end-user complaints and response times by 40 percent. As I was spearheading the SAP R/3 project systems enhancement and improvement initiative, a good friend and IT colleague reached out and challenged my leadership qualities with a request to accept an assignment on an engineering, procurement, and construction management (EPCM) project for a leading aluminum client in Russia. The focus of the assignment was to implement, support, and maintain for three project offices around the country a state-of-the-art local-area network (LAN), office automation, and integrated-project-delivery software suite.

The US $15 million investment effort covered a LAN consisting of twenty servers and 340 end users. The server environment included a Web front end for access to database and applications, external portal to allow vendors access to project documentation, database, active directory, e-mail, application for project-delivery software suite, and documentation filing. The infrastructure technology platform consisted of HP and Dell hardware, SQL database, Windows 2000 operating system, and Windows NT networks.

The four-month effort was about the implementation of a project-delivery suite of applications that included SAP R/3 version 4.6 c (time capturing and reporting), custom-developed cost control and progress management system, Primavera P3 (scheduling), document management system (OpenText LiveLink v9.0—document control and management), BMS's safety information management system, and Win Estimator (estimating). The support and maintenance team developed and implemented configuration, change-request, authorization, and disaster-recovery procedures. We also implemented and managed a support desk that enabled improved services, increased accuracy, increased availability of information, better management control, and improved management decision making.

When I stepped onto the international playing field, the importance of applying people-leadership qualities to following and maintaining agreed-upon business processes as a critical factor for system-implementation success dramatically impacted and molded the modified leader in me. The international business arena and the difficulty of mastering the local language put a new spin on team challenges, which included:

- IT and systems budget under client control
- No participation by implementation team in the budget-estimation effort
- IT infrastructure and accompanying administration team belonging to the client
- Part-time functional and technical support teams outside of project control
- Software systems not developed and tested to run in a client-infrastructure environment or support multiple joint-venture partner requirements
- Client requirements for process, function, and reporting not consistent with software design
- No business practices or supporting procedures agreed on before implementation and rollout
- EPCM management changes
- Difference in management style between locals and foreigners
- Failure by foreign management to fully understand the local legal requirements

Project 4. In June 2005, after a challenging fourteen months in Russia, I returned home to spend more time with family and took on the role of core-systems development lead, providing leadership and direction to the software development team and collaborating with the product-support team within the company to ensure that the required functionality and modifications were included in appropriate releases. In conjunction with product managers for the software vendor, we evaluated new technologies and products to determine the feasibility and desirability of incorporating their capabilities within the company core-system components.

Increased activity in the aluminum industry around the world raised the demand for system-implementation leadership skills, leading to me accepting the role of scoping, planning, and managing the implementation, support, and maintenance of a state-of-the-art integrated project-delivery software suite on an EPCM project for a leading aluminum client in Brazil.

The systems environment encompassed two locations, seven hundred end users, and twenty servers. The four-month, US$21 million system-implementation effort covered the implementation of a project-delivery software suite that included MARIAN (procurement, logistics, and materials management), SAP R/3 Projects (time management, project-breakdown structure, and invoicing), custom-developed engineering progress management system, custom-developed cost control system, document management system (OpenText—document control and management), and Primavera P5 (project scheduling). As part of the integration effort, the task also included the preparation, planning, and management of the implementation, support, and maintenance of a BizTalk integration platform, transferring data among four project delivery systems: MARIAN, iPAS, APMS (client system), and EBS-Oracle finance (client system). This time around, the new buzzword and technology introduced to the project was the implementation of a Web-based voice-and-video-over-IP communication platform called AliceStreet Conference Center.

Coming off the Russia project and going on to a second international assignment brought me to a strong realization that in non-first-world countries, the perception and belief exists that control is a proof of leadership and is required above all to bring project success. With a couple of minor exceptions, it seemed as if the international project-driven system implementations had very much the same challenges:

- IT and systems budget under client control
- No participation by implementation team in the budget-estimation effort
- IT infrastructure and accompanying administration team belonging to the client
- Part-time functional and technical support teams outside of project control
- Software systems not developed and tested to run in a client-infrastructure environment or support multiple joint-venture partner requirements
- Client requirements for process, function, and reporting not consistent with software design
- No business practices or supporting procedures agreed on before implementation and rollout
- EPCM management changes
- Difference in management style between locals and foreigners
- Failure by foreign management to fully understand the local legal requirements

Project 5. In August 2008, with my major international project assignments behind me, it was time to focus on and reconcile with my family. My relationship with my wife, Anna was increasingly strained, and my two wonderful daughters were grown up and on their way to university. It was time for me to keep my family together. In doing so, I had to change direction, travel less, and bring us all together in Vancouver.

While providing system-implementation management services to a molybdenum-mining client in British Columbia and a gold-mining client in Nunavut, Canada, I was asked by the Vancouver office management—because of my experience in EPCM project-delivery systems, understanding of project-delivery business function, and ability to lead diverse teams—to lead the EPCM project-delivery-services team. The team of approximately sixty professionals provided project-delivery services to all the mineral and mining processing and renewable-power projects in the Vancouver office. I provided leadership to specialists in the following areas: project setup, accounting and time management (SAP R/3 version 4.6 c), capital cost estimating (Candy), planning and scheduling (Primavera P6), procurement and materials management (MARIAN), project cost control (custom-developed application), engineering progress (custom-developed application), and document management and control (OpenText LiveLink version 9.0). Special assigned tasks included optimization of business processes, procedures, computerized tools-that-work, and team and business-functions productivity.

After two major international assignments, I had hoped for a smooth ride and was pleasantly surprised by the variety and large number of challenges that the team faced in implementing and using the various project-delivery systems. The project-delivery-services team's leadership skills and qualities were challenged by:

- Project-delivery systems that were mainly developed for the mineral and mining processing industry and not for the renewable power industry
- Renewable power projects that were small in dollar value, stretching over a large time duration
- Conflicting reporting requirements between project managers and business management
- The perception of project managers that the corporate systems were designed for large EPCM projects
- The need for project managers to accept the various corporate systems
- Project managers' perception that software systems were only databases and, like spreadsheets, easily manipulated
- Human resources that were shared among the different projects in the office
- Shared resources that, at the same time, had to deal with different project-management philosophies, system releases, system configurations, processes and procedures, and phases of the project
- System support that depended on remote resources
- Functional-support teams finding it difficult to configure the various systems to cater to the medium to smaller projects
- Project managers' and clients' inability to adjust and accept the standard (company-wide) reports
- Corporate development teams that were slow in responding to system-functionality enhancements
- Realization that it was not possible to always adjust the systems to suit a specific environment or application

It is these real-life experiences since 1996 that have allowed me to develop the leadership quality matrix and my modified leadership style. The cube below demonstrates the three dimensions of the leadership quality matrix.

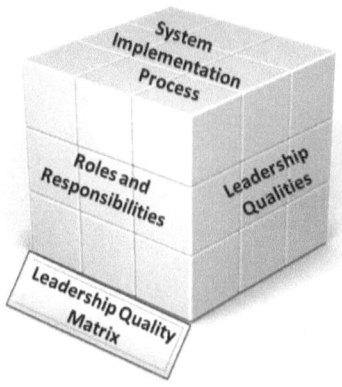

Figure 1.1: Dimensions of Leadership Quality Matrix

The cube demonstrates the fact that, though there is a fixed set of stakeholders, implementation processes, and leadership qualities, the requirements will change as the combination where they stand in relation to each other changes.

As we, in information system implementations, so many times refer to road maps, I will make use of a trip analogy to explain the layout of this book. Section one is about getting ready to undertake the trip. In this section, I elaborate on who the key stakeholders are from both an organizational and project perspectives and the roles and responsibilities they have on the system-implementation project. I also provide a system-implementation road map that explains the system-implementation process required.

Section two focuses on the trip. This section of the book focuses on turning the cube to align for each implementation process the correct roles and responsibilities and link to those the required leadership qualities. As a matter of fact, this section is the leadership quality matrix.

Section three is the instruments available to prepare for the trip. This section focuses on the various leadership models that are available to assist recruitment specialists to determine if potential team members have leadership qualities as defined by the leadership quality matrix.

With an understanding of the challenging system implementations that have molded the modified leader in me, the first step in formulating the leadership quality matrix is to get an understanding of and focus on the key stakeholders responsible to provide the required roles, responsibilities, and leadership qualities.

Chapter Two

Stakeholders

Topic Introduction

The first step in putting together the leadership quality matrix is to clearly define the various stakeholders and the roles and responsibilities they have on the system-implementation project. As the success of any information-system implementation equally depends on both the organization and the implementation team, the process starts with identifying the structure and roles and responsibilities of both the organizational team and the project team.

Organizational Team

Although on different types of system implementations the required roles and responsibilities will slightly differ and also be differently implemented, the following organizational roles are required, to a greater or lesser extent, on all projects:

> *Senior management*
> *Executive sponsor*
> *Business -process owner*
> *Business -functional expert*
> *End user*
> *Service and support team*

To get an understanding of the workload of the various positions, I'll provide an experience-based description of these organization-team positions:

Senior management. The senior management team—sometimes referred to as top or upper management—is generally a team of individuals at the highest level of organizational management who have the day-to-day responsibilities of managing the organization. From a system-implementation perspective, the primary responsibilities of senior management are:

- Promoting the system implementation throughout the organization
- Motivating end users to adopt and adapt to the newly implemented system
- Motivating end users to employ the newly implemented system in the way it was designed to function

Executive sponsor. The executive sponsor, traditionally a member of senior management, communicates regarding the company's business activities and focuses the system implementation on the company's long-term goals and visions. As ultimate owner of the system implementation, the executive sponsor's primary responsibilities are:

- Decision making in the fulfillment of the team's primary responsibilities, as outlined by the steering committee
- Maintaining the final authority to set priorities, approve scope, and settle company-wide issues
- Promoting the system implementation throughout the organization, negotiating solutions where conflicts exist
- Having the final budget authority

Business-process owner. The business-process owner has responsibility for the business process for a specific area from a strategic point of view. He or she works directly with the business-process team lead and team members to communicate the success factors associated with specific business-process areas. The business-process owner approves the system solution for an assigned business area. From my experience, the business-process owner is one of the most critical positions for a successful system rollout and has the following primary responsibilities:

- Ensuring business targets and objectives are met by the system
- Working with the project-team leader to develop the "to be" view of the business processes
- Planning change-management activities for existing business processes as necessary
- Identifying and managing mission-critical business scenarios
- Validating expected results versus actual results

Business-functional expert. The business-functional expert's key focus is the execution of the detailed design and configuration of the company's business processes within the new system. The business-functional experts ensure that the system is doing what it is supposed to do, with the following key responsibilities:

- Working with the project team leader in the analysis and decomposition of the business processes, documenting the business-process requirements, and designing and configuring the system to support the organization's "to be" process vision
- Aiding in the design of reports, forms, interfaces, and conversions
- Executing the system unit and integration testing, which includes performing the test, making changes in configuration based on results, and resolving errors
- Conducting workshops and presentations to validate business processes and system solutions with the end-user community
- Working with the end-user-documentation developers and trainers in the identification of business-processes and technical-system tasks to be documented
- Providing training to the end-user training team

Because of the importance of the business-functional expert position, I'll highlight some of the characteristics the successful candidate should have:

- Sharing experience as a current system user or technical-support representative
- Sharing experience as an information-systems analyst with strong business application knowledge or a business-application analyst with strong technical proficiency
- Making decisions on functional, process, or operational changes
- Acting on in-depth knowledge of the company's business processes, balanced with strong analytical skills
- Being an excellent team player, with strong oral and written communication skills
- Making decisions under time constraints
- Showing a balanced mix of skills—driver and facilitator, visionary and doer
- Having experience with system implementations, conducting presentations, and training
- Possessing advanced application-software skills, including presentation, spreadsheet, and word-processing applications

End user. The end user is the person who, on a day-to-day basis, performs his or her work by using the implemented system. The key responsibilities of end users, though simple, are nonnegotiable and high-risk to the business, and include:

- Partaking in system-integration testing
- Using a newly implemented system in the way it was designed to function
- Adopting together with the implemented systems the applicable business process

Service and support team. The service and support team is responsible for providing both application and technical support to power users and the end-user community during the day-to-day use of the system. Usually this role is fulfilled by business-process and technical team members for the initial go-live and production support. Service and support providers are the first line of help for all questions or problems during the company's daily business. Individual questions and issues have to be analyzed and classified. If members of the service and support team cannot resolve the problem, they will forward it to the business-functional expert. The service and support team leader establishes the procedures and organizes a team to support end users during production operations. Responsibilities include:

- Defining help-desk support strategy for go-live and operations
- Defining and setting up service and support logging database
- Coordinating with project-management team in assignment of resources to the help desk
- Day-to-day managing of help-desk activities and monitoring of response and problems logged

Project Team

As with the organizational team on different types of system implementations, the project-team roles and responsibilities may differ slightly and be differently implemented. The following project-team roles, to a more or lesser extent, are required on all projects:

> *System-implementation manager*
> *Team leader*
> *Integration manager*
> *Functional consultant*
> *Technical consultant*
> *Key user*

To get an understanding of the workload of the various positions, I'll provide an experience-based description of each.

System-implementation manager. The system-implementation manager assists in the definition and execution of project deliverables and the day-to-day management of the entire project. I strongly prefer a system-implementation manager who is on the company payroll; he or she does not need technical know-how but rather functional business-process and analytical experience. The responsibilities of the system-implementation manager include:

- Acting as the main liaison for the team members with the steering committee, project sponsor, and partner management

- Providing methodology for implementation approach
- Assisting project-management and project team in internalizing the implementation road map
- Aiding in the definition of project deliverables and critical target dates to be reflected in the project plan
- Assisting in the definition of project scope and objectives
- Aiding in the resolution of issues when necessary
- Assisting consultants and individual teams when necessary in the completion of tasks
- Ongoing management of project resources

Team leader. The selection of the most suitable team leaders is a critical factor in implementation success. From a system-implementation perspective, the individual with the most application knowledge in each functional area should act as team leader. To be successful, both functional and technical team leaders are required. On larger and more complex implementations, the technical team leader is also known as the systems architect. The primary responsibilities of the team leader are:

- Managing the completion of all assigned project deliverables
- Providing expert knowledge and direction to the team or group
- Setting up and configuring high-risk areas
- Working with system-implementation manager to plan the scope, schedule, budget, and resources
- Working with business-process owner to ensure that the system will support the envisioned business process
- Working with functional experts to ensure that the system is doing what it is supposed to do

Integration manager. The SAP integration manager is responsible for coordinating cross-team activities within SAP. He or she is concerned with ensuring that the elements making up a project are properly coordinated so that project goals are achieved. The primary responsibilities of the integration manager are:

- Providing leadership to major IT and systems initiatives that are cross-functional

- Making tradeoffs between competing or conflicting cross-team objectives
- Coordinating all functional departments for efficiency and effectiveness
- Facilitating software integration of all business functions
- Embracing the versatility and functionality of the SAP software to create business solutions

Functional consultant. The functional consultant is an application expert. In larger systems, such as SAP R/3, the functional consultant might be focused on a specific module or function. The primary responsibilities of the functional consultant are:

- Configuring the application, module, or function
- Transferring knowledge of system design and configuration to team members
- Providing knowledge of best business practices to aid the design process
- Acting as advisor and aiding the project team in all tasks as necessary.

Technical consultant. Depending on the size and complexity of the system implementation, the team might require one or more technical consultants to cover certain areas of expertise, such as system administration, database administration, network administration, operating-system administration, cross-application development, or software-language-specific development. The primary responsibilities of the technical consultant are:

- Performing installation, setup, and configuration of the applicable technical environment
- Transferring technical expertise to service and support teams
- Offering guidance and advice for all technical aspects of the system implementation
- Providing technical day-to-day direction, including detecting project deviations and taking immediate corrective action
- Developing and managing the cut-over plan prior to going live and production startup

- Acting as the communication link with the IT operation centers

Key user. The key user is a resource identified and assigned by management to the project based on specific knowledge of the country, region, site, function, or application. On an informal basis, the key user can be seen as the leader of a specific end-user community and also the most knowledgeable member. The key user is responsible for:

- Providing the project-team members with all the required site-specific information, documentation, and data for the successful implementation of the system
- Participating in workshops and presentations to validate the system design being implemented
- Working with the project-team leader in the identification of end-user documentation and end-user training requirements at his or her particular site
- Conducting end-user training
- Working with the programmers and layout developers to validate the sources of data and resulting converted data, and design and output forms and reports

From a Modified Leader's Pen

Based on my years of experience in this process and systems implementation leadership, my fundamental belief is that what is required from team members to positively impact the system-implementation process is more important than the system-implementation process itself. It is clear to me that as system-implementation managers and information-systems specialists, it is our responsibility to act as change agents, addressing the perception that leadership is a management function only.

Over the last decade, a large number of studies have been performed by scientists like Henry Mintzberg focusing on the application of the leadership role in organizations and on projects. Looking around in the business environment, I have to agree with the findings of Manfred Kets de Vries (2001:73), a well-published clinical professor of leadership development, that in general, the leadership role is applied in one of three ways:

- Leaders as figureheads
- Leaders as movers of life-size chess pieces
- Leaders as individuals who speak to the collective imagination of their people and thereby co-opt them to join the journey

For system implementations to be managed in an orderly fashion, it is important that the organization select a system-implementation manager who can speak to the collective imagination of all the team members. Furthermore, the organization should allow the system-implementation manager full control over his or her destiny and the destiny of the team, and he or she should have the freedom to select and motivate team members to their full commitment and extra effort.

A system-implementation manager who wants to create and lead a team needs to understand the dynamics of leadership. This is not to minimize such factors as scope, the position in terms of other ongoing projects, or the team's extensive technology capabilities. These factors are important for sure, but they're not as important as leadership. If the leadership dimension is properly established, the system implementation can and will be successful.

Leadership guru Manfred Kets de Vries defines the components that contribute to leadership effectiveness as the personalistic and the situational (Kets de Vries, 2001:215).

$$\left\{ \begin{array}{c} \underline{\textbf{Leadership Effectiveness}} \\ \text{Personalistic component = personality variables} \\ \text{Situational component = environmental constraints} \\ \\ \underline{\textbf{Personalistic Contributor s}} \\ \text{Property = Behavior patterns and personality attributes} \\ \text{Process = Drawing on various bases of power to influence a group} \end{array} \right\}$$

The personalistic contributors are focused on the specific personality variables that impact and determine leadership effectiveness, while the situational contributors represent the environmental constraints on leadership effectiveness.

I strongly believe that, though environmental constraints play an important role in system implementations, it is the unique leadership personality variables of each team member that allow for successful control and management of the environmental constraints.

Manfred Kets de Vries has broken down the personalistic component of effective leadership into two contributors: property and process. **Property leadership** refers to a set of characteristics—behavior pattern and personality attributes—that make certain people more effective than others at attaining a set of goals. **Process leadership**, on the other hand, refers to an effort by a leader who is drawing on various bases of power to influence members of a group to direct their activities toward a common goal.

During the team selection process, it is important to keep the environmental constraints, such as behaviors of functional managers and where people are placed in an organizational structure, in mind to ensure that the selected resources have the correct mix in terms of behavior patterns and personality attributes.

To be right the first time in the selection of the correct mix of team members at the beginning of the project is becoming more and more important as the pressure on system implementations to derive return on investment on a daily basis becomes more and more intense. The implication of this is that the time allowed for adjustments to the individual change process (concern, confrontation, clarification, crystallization, and change) or the organizational change process (creating a shared mind-set; changing behavior; building competencies, practices, and attitudes; and improving business performance) has been reduced significantly.

My success to date comes from the fact that, as a leader, I always attempt to speak to the collective imagination of my team and to focus on the personality variables in my team rather than environmental constraints. In my selection of and dealing with team members, my focus is always on their personality and behavior. In leading system implementations, I prefer to draw on the various bases of power to influence the team. In 1959, two psychologists, John French and Bertman Raven, identified five bases of power (Kalyan City Life Blog, August 30, 2011):

- Legitimate power—A person's right to make demands and expect compliance and obedience from others
- Reward power—A person's ability to compensate another for compliance or performance
- Expert power—A person's superior skill and knowledge

- Referent power—A person's perceived attractiveness, worthiness. and right to respect from others
- Coercive power—A person's ability to punish others for noncompliance

As a modified leader, I have learned that, though you have to be consistent and fair toward all team members, you have to understand and focus on each team member separately as well. Let me explain. On one of the projects where I worked, there was salary disparity between the consultants and seconded organizational team members. Due to my position in the organization, I could call on my reward power to bring salaries in-line, which helped to improve the productivity and quality of work. On the same project, I had a team member who was not willing to comply with project time lines, and I had to call on my coercive power to replace the individual. When it comes to leadership and the use of the five bases of power, it is important for the leader to also understand and recognize the power that each team member possesses, realize what bases of power should be developed in each individual team member, and understand how individual team members are impacted by the various bases of power.

I want to conclude by saying that one real issue for me as a system-implementation leader is the commitment of the team members to the project time lines and objectives. As a modified leader, I seldom call on my coercive power to lead a team; but at the same time, I have to say that, though a team member might have all the personality variables and the skills that are required, unless that team member commits, he or she must move on and be replaced by members who are willing and committed.

As part of getting ready to undertake the trip, in this section I have elaborated on who the key stakeholders from both an organizational and project perspectives are and the roles and responsibilities they have on the system-implementation project.

In the next chapter, I deal with the system-implementation road map that explains the system-implementation process required.

Chapter Three

Implementation Process

Topic Introduction

With the various key stakeholders and their roles and responsibilities defined, this section focuses on the second fundamental component in putting together the leadership quality matrix: a definition of the implementation process.

The focus on the implementation process stems from the realization that it is not always possible to adjust the systems to suit a specific environment or application, and that the answer lies in the implementation process and the people using the applications.

Focusing on the implementation process is important to ensure that all stakeholders are paying attention to and driving toward the same outcome. Leadership qualities are more easily assigned to some implementation processes than others, and these processes also have a higher certainty of success.

The figure below outlines the traditional system-implementation road map:

Information System Implementations: Using a Leadership Quality Matrix for Success

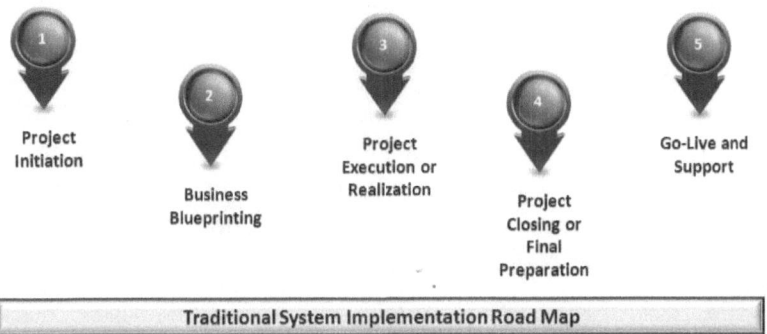

Figure 3.1: Traditional System-Implementation Road Map

Though the names of the five phases differ among systems implementation integrators, the work to be done is similar in nature. Based on experience and information published by Pinto and Millet (1999), by following the traditional system-implementation road map:

- The budgetary and schedule breakdowns are as follows: project preparation, 6 percent; business blueprinting, 28 percent; realization, 45 percent; final preparation, 15 percent; and go-live and support, 6 percent.
- The activities that make up each of these phases are defined by what is to be done, why it is needed, how it is to be performed, and who should implement it.

From my experience, this viewpoint, because of its technical focus, makes it extremely difficult to select and assign resources with the correct leadership qualities. The phased approach is also more focused on group work and is of limited value in the selection and assigning of people. Furthermore, it is clear that the current system-implementation road maps are focused on the computer programs to be configured—the customization or enhancement of a specific application—and not directly on the business results to be accomplished.

This technical focus is actually understandable. Manfred Kets de Vries explains that from a theoretical perspective, organizational specialists, because of human nature, give structure and systems precedence over people (2001:221). One of the most logical explanations for this outlook is that structures and systems are much easier to deal with.

People are much more complex and hard to change. Special attention and continuous focus on people are critical to overcoming the existing theoretical perspective.

The importance of a more people-oriented focus became obvious during the mid-1990s when the major enterprise-software development houses started investing a significant amount of time and effort in improving applications by addressing various implementations, implementation methodology, and people-related issues.

- Baan Consulting stressed that when it comes to software implementations, vision, focus, and a fast time to value are key. Baan developed an implementation process based on a methodology that works and is executed by people who understand the client's business objectives. Baan strived to bring dedicated, certified business and application professionals to each and every enterprise-system implementation.
- PeopleSoft started to focus on customer organizations with fast, predictable, and low-risk results, through highly trained and experienced consultants working worldwide and tailored methodologies for implementing, upgrading, and optimizing enterprise system implementations.
- J. D. Edwards, one of the world's leading developers of agile software solutions, focused its attention on providing customers with what they need to compete in today's connected world by integrating and facilitating any conceivable business process and making customer-enterprise system implementations more responsive, more efficient, and more profitable.
- SAP AG took responsibility for the success of client solutions throughout the implementation life cycle. It brought together SAP experts, product development, and certified partners to provide a single point of contact and consistent services and methodologies around the world.

This direction of the major enterprise-systems development houses is understandable because seven of the success factors critical to system-implementation success, as identified by Pinto and Millet's ten-factor model (Pinto and Millet, 1999:54), are people-related factors. The ten-factor model includes:

- **Project mission.** Initial clearly defined goals and general direction
- **Top management support.** The willingness of top management to provide the necessary resources and authority/power to make the implementation a success
- **Schedule/plans.** Detailed specification of the individual action steps for system implementation
- **Client consultation.** Communication, consultation, and active listening to all parties impacted by the proposed information system
- **Personnel.** Recruitment, selection, and training of necessary personnel for the implementation project team
- **Technical tasks.** Availability of the required technology and expertise to accomplish the specific technical action steps to bring the information system online
- **Client acceptance.** Act of selling the final product to its ultimate intended users
- **Monitoring and feedback.** Timely provision of comprehensive control information at each stage in the implementation process
- **Communication.** Provision of an appropriate network and necessary data to all key actors in the information-system implementation process
- **Troubleshooting.** Ability to handle unexpected crises and deviations from plans

From a Modified Leader's Pen

My national and international system implementations and the challenges that they brought have taught me that critical success factors can and should be derived directly from the system-implementation strategy. Based on the various system implementations and their challenges over the past twelve years, I have identified the following as the most critical factors for system implementations (which, in broad terms, are very similar to the Pinto and Millet ten-factor model):

- Quick decision making from all leaders
- Resource availability
- Leadership support
- Minimal systems customization

- Strong scope and deliverable management
- Effective communication
- Proven implementation methodology
- Balanced and well-selected system-implementation team
- Ground rules for team interaction
- Vendor relationship management
- Effective change management
- System-implementation leadership

Working through the mentioned critical success factors, I have realized that, because of the pressure on system-implementation teams to realize value to the business, the traditional phased approach is no longer a workable methodology. Realizing value to the business more quickly means taking the least amount of time from system implementation to system operations, with an emphasis on the following series of chronological tasks: project management, process standardization, transition from the initial system-configuration exercise to system-operation life cycle, benefit realization, and troubleshooting during both the project and system-operation life cycle. The figure below outlines the chronological series of tasks that further on in the publication will be used as system-implementation process focus areas.

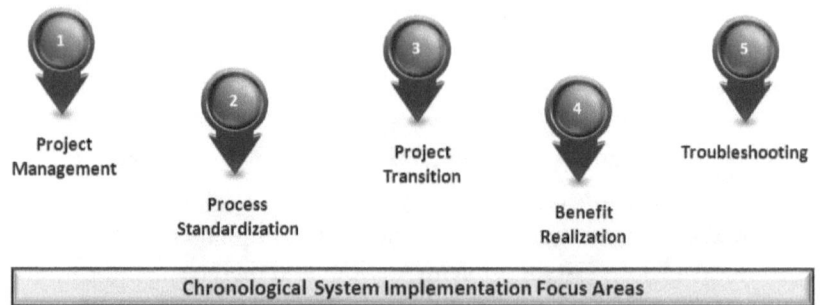

Figure 3.2: Chronological System-Implementation Focus Areas

Obviously, these implementation-process focus areas are focused on what has to be achieved, what the business impact will be, and what leadership qualities are required. This will assist the team in keeping the focus on the elements that help system implementations deliver value to the business throughout the implementation and across more than one of the traditional phases at a specific time. In the following chapters, we'll look at each of these focus areas in more detail.

This marks the end of the getting ready to undertake the trip section. Section two is about the trip. The trip refers to the leadership quality matrix. Chapters four to eight focus on turning the cube to align for each implementation process focus area the correct roles and responsibilities and link to those the required leadership qualities. As indicated, this as a matter of fact is the leadership quality matrix.

Section Two

The Trip

Chapter Four

Project Management

Topic Introduction

The first implementation-process focus area that requires our attention is project management. Unlike the other four implementation-process focus areas, project management spans the full duration of the system implementation from start to finish.

The importance not only for the organization but for the project-management team lies in the fact that, unlike a manufacturing or production environment with repetitive processes and multiple outputs, system implementation brings the uniqueness of a onetime endeavor. The outcome of this onetime endeavor—with a group of tasks to be performed in a definable time period to meet a specific set of objectives—is either success or failure.

The project-management effort is a group rather than a single-person effort. It depends heavily on the experience and competency of team members in executing the following tasks: scope, time, cost, communication, human resources, contract and procurement, construction, and integration. I am taking the time to describe each of the mentioned tasks as they define the required roles, responsibilities, and leadership qualities for the project-management process. Furthermore, addressing these tasks early in the project establishes a solid foundation for a successful implementation and ensures that it proceeds efficiently.

- **Scope management.** The system-implementation scope can be defined as the sum total of the work (including requirements and features) to be performed. Most of the time, the scope of a project is best described by the work breakdown structure and work descriptions. Scope management refers to the process of controlling and documenting the scope and changes.
- **Time management.** Because the project has a fixed duration and is set in the context of a finite period of time, activities are planned and scheduled to suit.
- **Cost management.** Effective financial control of the project must be monitored relative to the objectives.
- **Communication management.** Organizing and conducting the exchange of information, both internally and externally, is essential to successful system implementation.
- **Human-resources management.** Administrative and behavioral knowledge are employed throughout the life of a project to assemble, direct, and coordinate human resources. Projects are achieved through people and their respective skills and abilities.
- **Contract and procurement management.** The end product depends on resources acquired through some form of formal contract.
- **Construction management.** Resources must be assembled and directed to build the end product or facility.
- **Integration management.** Integration management involves the management of activities such as planning, organizing, directing, and monitoring, applied simultaneously to all the above functions.

From a Modified Leader's Pen

The timely preparation of the system-implementation project plan and addressing of project-plan-related issues during the course of the project require continuous input and leadership from the following stakeholders:

$$\left\{ \begin{array}{c} \textit{System-implementation manager} \\ \textit{Team leaders} \\ \textit{Executive sponsor} \end{array} \right\}$$

System-Implementation Manager

As system-implementation management spans all phases of the project, it is important that the system-implementation manager become aware of the team's needs on a constant basis and be available to help them. It is wrong to expect the system-implementation manager to be Mister Tough Guy—or, for that matter, Girl.

The system-implementation manager needs to have the following leadership qualities:

Servanthood
Competence
Communication
Character
Commitment
Passion
Courage
Judgment
Problem solving

Servanthood. In serving both the project-team members and the organizational structure, the system-implementation manager must put their needs before his or her own agenda.

Competence. In dealing with multiple sites, multiple locations, and different time zones, the system-implementation manager has the task of inspiring the various project and organizational teams to deliver tasks on time.

Communication. Those multiple sites, multiple locations, and different time zones also require the system-implementation manager to have exceptional leadership skills in communication. He or she must act as a link between the project team and the organization in terms of understanding what needs to be communicated and translating the message in a way the organization will understand.

Character. The project can only succeed if the system-implementation manager has the ability to rally both the project and the organization team members to a common purpose. If team members refuse to participate and accept the challenge, they should be replaced sooner rather than later.

Commitment. The system-implementation manager's contribution must go beyond serving the various project and organization team members, opening doors that will allow them to execute their assigned activities and achieve their project objectives and goals.

Passion. It is the system-implementation manager's passion that will allow for a successful implementation in a very short time frame. An eight-hour-a-day system-implementation manager just does not work for rapid system implementations.

Courage. The system-implementation manager must seek solutions for the long run and not only as an interim measure.

Judgment. Finding the root of problems in order to solve them for the long run is a responsibility that falls to the system-implementation manager.

Problem solving. Realizing the big picture is important for successful completion of rapid system implementation. I am against system-implementation managers with specialized technical skills because they have trouble seeing beyond their area of expertise. Also, in most situations, that expertise results in conflict with technical-team leaders or the danger of confusing the two roles. When I read advertisements for system-implementation manager positions and technical skills are listed as a requirement, it's a clear indication that the advertiser does not understand the work of leadership on projects. The system-implementation manager is not there to do the technical configuration.

Team Leaders

Team leaders for each of the application modules of relevance must have the technical skills to support the various team members. The system-implementation team leader in particular is required to have high levels of technical, functional, and management skills. Based on the mentioned skills, the following leadership qualities are called for:

Responsibility
Courage
Self-discipline
Judgment
Problem solving

Responsibility. It is expected that the project-team leader will show leadership in getting tasks done within the agreed framework. If the project-team leader cannot or does not want to accept set time frames, please replace; he or she will be a stumbling block.

Courage. The system-implementation team leader's courage to get the job done inspires the individual team members to also deliver.

Self-discipline. Very early in the project, the system-implementation team leaders must show signs that they are willing to challenge their own and their teams' excuses. If not, they will not be able to deliver tasks within the agreed-upon time frame.

Judgment. Once again, the project-team leader is the most knowledgeable person in his or her area of specialty and should at all times evaluate the design for maximum impact. This is true from both a system and a business perspective.

Problem solving. With the high level of technical skills required in the specific areas, the team leaders should anticipate problems that might lead to an unsuccessful design, and do so very early and not only during the testing phase.

Executive Sponsor

The project-management process is highly dependent on the input of the executive sponsor as a member of the most senior organization team. From the executive sponsor are required the following leadership qualities:

Commitment. The executive sponsor's commitment to the global project is what opens doors for successful implementation.

Vision. It is the vision of the executive sponsor that helps in gathering project and organization resources for a rapid system implementation.

All Project Team Members

Besides the specific individual leadership qualities identified above, I am of the opinion that the success of short-duration system implementations (both the project and operations life cycle) depends on having a stakeholder community that is striving toward the leadership goals outlined by Peter Urs Bender in his book *Leadership from Within* (1977): seek fulfillment, make progress, and create results.

Seek fulfillment. It is not about how many projects, tasks, or decisions the team members complete, but how much satisfaction they get out of the projects, tasks, or decisions they complete. You need passion for life, for completion, for the software product.

Make progress. Team members must have the leadership qualities to set goals themselves, to lead them from where they are to where they and the team should be. They need to have internal motivation, to take responsibility and do things themselves without being told to do so. Team members with the ability and will to develop a wider range of skills can do more than what they are contracted for.

Create results. Team members need to have the right attitude and behavior-leadership qualities to complete short-duration global implementations. Thus, team members should have the ability to make choices in order to cope with the complexities around the project and to express their intentions on coping with the complexities around short-duration global system implementations.

Assessing Your Project-Management Quotient

Based on the definition of the first system-implementation focus area (project management), the identified roles and responsibilities, and the assigned leadership qualities, I provide below a list of questions or phrases that can be used during the identification, selection, and placement of team members.

System-Implementation Manager

Spend time with the potential or proposed system-implementation manager and determine if the person possesses the following leadership qualities:

- **Servanthood.** Inquire as to the last time acts of kindness were performed.
- **Competence.** Reevaluate standards to ensure consistent performance on high levels.
- **Communication.** Examine recently written letters or memos to get a feel for clarity and simplicity.
- **Character.** Identify weaknesses or problems that keep on surfacing.
- **Commitment.** See if the individual understands how plans are made public and follows through with them.
- **Passion.** Find out about all major areas of life the individual is involved in (work, marriage, family, service, projects).
- **Courage.** Determine what has been done to get people to compromise and work together.
- **Judgment.** Ask about the last time the experiences learned have been used.
- **Problem solving.** Understand the actions taken to continually see the big picture, avoid being overwhelmed by emotion, not get bogged down in details, and keep track of what is important.

Team Leaders

Spend time with the potential or proposed team leader and determine if the person possesses the following leadership qualities:

- **Responsibility.** Understand actions taken to overcome persistent problems.
- **Courage.** Observe activities that have stretched abilities and caused the individual to feel afraid.
- **Self-discipline.** Determine the reasons (excuses) for not following through with priorities.
- **Judgment.** Ask about the last time a task has been evaluated for maximum impact.
- **Problem solving.** Assess the size and frequency of problems that have been dealt with.

Executive Sponsor

Spend time with the potential or proposed executive sponsor and determine if the person possesses the following leadership qualities:

- **Commitment.** See if actions performed match his or her ideals.
- **Vision.** Observe actions taken to attract, challenge, and unite resources.

All Project Team Members

Spend time with the potential or proposed team member and determine if the person possesses the following goal-oriented leadership qualities:

- **Seek fulfillment.** Determine how much satisfaction the team member gets out of the projects, tasks, or decisions he completes.
- **Make progress.** Understand the ability of the team member to set goals himself, to lead from where he is to where he should be.
- **Create results.** Find out if the team member has the right attitude and behavior to complete short-duration global implementations.

Paying attention to material outlined by the Modified Leader's Pen and the Project-Management Quotient sections will allow the system-implementation manager and recruitment specialists to:

- Select the appropriate stakeholders to perform the roles and responsibilities for the project management focus area of the system implementation.
- Know the leadership qualities for each of the identified roles.
- Ask the right questions to determine if the potential team members possess the required leadership qualities.

Chapter five will focus on turning the cube to align for the process standardization focus area the correct roles and responsibilities and link to those the required leadership qualities.

Chapter Five

Process Standardization

Topic Introduction

The second implementation-process focus area we will focus on is standardization. Based on the traditional system-implementation road map, the business process of standardization is shaped during the second and third phases. During the business-blueprinting phase, a common understanding is established between the business and project team; and then during the realization phase, the project team translates its understanding of the business-process requirements through system configuration into a single business system.

The business-blueprinting phase has as its goal to produce a document (and in some situations a prototype) detailing the business process agreed upon during the various requirement workshops. The business blueprint not only documents the company's agreed-upon business-process requirements, but also provides insight into how the organization intends to run its business on a global basis. From a system-implementation perspective, the business-blueprinting phase refines the original project goals and objectives, defines the baseline scope, and refines the overall project schedule and implementation sequence.

During the realization phase, the system-implementation team transforms the business-process concepts formulated as requirements during the blueprinting phase into a workable system. The success of realization-phase activities depends on the extent to which the project team can build on the knowledge gained during the business-blueprinting phase. The realization-phase activities are executed on a package-work breakdown that is schedule-driven. The core areas of concern during the realization phase are performing the system configuration and/or application development, performing an overall test, and releasing the system into production.

To achieve a common understanding and to ensure the system is functioning the way it should, it is important to have the same resources involved and manage both the mentioned tasks as a single continuous action.

From a Modified Leader's Pen

The leadership skills required during process standardization are of the utmost importance—because of the completeness required of documentation, research, meeting facilitation, and getting consensus and agreement, as well as the time-consuming and tiring nature of the task at hand.

During the standardization of business processes, in order to address the issues of multiple countries, multiple companies and business units, and cultural and governmental differences in a timely manner, specific leadership skills are required from the following stakeholders:

$$\left\{ \begin{array}{c} \textit{Business-process owner} \\ \textit{Business-functional experts} \\ \textit{Functional and technical consultants} \\ \textit{Key users} \end{array} \right\}$$

Business-Process Owner

The owner of the business process for a specific business function has to lead the global process-standardization exercise. Unlike the other roles, this one requires continuous focus past the point of project completion. The business-process owner should have the following leadership qualities:

Character. The process owner has to be well trusted and without major shortfalls that will prevent the organization from following the business process after completion of the project.

Commitment. Proven leadership skills in opening doors to achieve success, from getting access to the correct resources through arranging time to meet with senior management, are important from the process owner.

Courage. The process owner must have the authority and the willingness to straighten out problems or stumbling blocks when they occur.

Vision. Reaching beyond personal experience and expertise, the process owner should possess company and international business vision.

Business-Functional Experts

The process owner depends on the business-functional experts to assist with the business-process standardization. Where the business-process owner is focused on the future vision, the business-functional experts are focused on day-to-day function execution. Business-functional experts need the following leadership qualities:

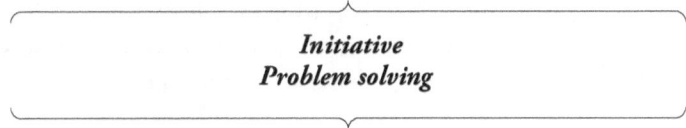

Initiative. Functional experts effectively utilize the scarce time of the people who know what has to be done to produce a successful business-process blueprint.

Problem solving. The functional experts should have the ability to anticipate problems that can occur because of standardization or a specific design.

Functional and Technical Consultants

With the configuration activity in mind, the first project-team roles from which exceptional leadership skills are required during business-process standardization are the functional and technical consultants. The team is depending on the functional and technical consultants, who normally are external to the organization, for the following leadership qualities:

Responsibility
Competence

Responsibility. During a global implementation, the team is looking for consultants who take responsibility for producing a successful application based on standardized business processes.

Competence. Consultants must be willing to stay within the agreed financial framework and do more than what is expected of them.

Key Users

Besides the functional and technical consultants, the key users are the other important group from which special leadership qualities are required. In comparison with the functional and technical consultants, the key users are secondary; but post-project, the business will look to them for effective and efficient execution. The team and the business will expect the following leadership qualities from key users:

Judgment
Responsibility

Judgment. Together with the business-functional experts, key users determine the maximum impact of the business-standardization process and design.

Responsibility. Key users must willingly take responsibility for getting the job done—not looking at the system-implementation manager to drive the project but making it their own.

Assessing Your Project-Management Quotient

Based on the definition of the second system-implementation focus area (process standardization), the identified roles and responsibilities, and the assigned leadership qualities, I provide below a list of questions or phrases that can be used during the identification, selection, and placement of team members.

Business-Process Owner

Spend time with the potential or proposed business-process owner and determine if the person possesses the following leadership qualities:

- **Character.** Utilize diagnostic instruments to identify detectable weakness or problem patterns.
- **Commitment.** Determine if actions match ideals.
- **Courage.** Understand what has been done to get people to compromise and work together.
- **Vision:** Ask the individual about the impact of his or her vision.

Business-Functional Experts

Spend time with the potential or proposed business-functional expert and determine if the person possesses the following leadership qualities:

- **Initiative.** Understand to what extent they are going to seek out opportunities.
- **Problem solving.** Ask about the biggest and most frequent problems they have had to deal with.

Functional and Technical Consultants

Spend time with the potential or proposed functional and technical consultants and determine if each person possesses the following leadership qualities:

- **Responsibility.** Understand what the individual is doing to achieve excellence.
- **Competence.** Determine what the individual is doing to reevaluate standards and ensure that he or she is performing consistently at high levels.

Key Users

Spend time with the potential or proposed key user and determine if the person possesses the following leadership qualities:

- **Judgment.** Ask about the last time the individual used his or her gut feeling and the experience gained.
- **Responsibility.** Understand what actions have been taken to overcome persistent problems.

Paying attention to material outlined by the Modified Leader's Pen and the Project-Management Quotient sections will allow the system-implementation manager and recruitment specialists to:

- Select the appropriate stakeholders to perform the roles and responsibilities for the process standardization focus area of the system implementation.
- Know the leadership qualities for each of the identified roles.
- Ask the right questions to determine if the potential team members possess the required leadership qualities.

Chapter six will focus on turning the cube to align for the project transition focus area the correct roles and responsibilities and link to those the required leadership qualities.

Chapter Six

Project Transition

Topic Introduction

The third implementation-process focus area that requires our attention is transitioning. Transition refers to the move from the old business processes to the new and also from the old applications to the new or enhanced applications.

Interestingly enough, based on the traditional system-implementation road map, the system-implementation transitioning happens during two stages—first during the final preparation phase of the project life cycle, and second during the go-live and support phase.

In reality, one can argue that transitioning in the case of an existing system that only requires configuration changes has already started during the realization phase. This is correct from a traditional perspective, but from my experience, including the realization phase complicates the assigning of resources and leadership qualities.

The purpose of the final preparation phase is to finalize your readiness to go live, including testing, end-user training, system management, and cut-over activities. The final preparation phase also provides an opportunity to resolve all crucial open issues. Upon successful completion of this phase, the implementation team will have a system ready to move into production.

The operations phase follows the final preparation phase. The purpose of the operations phase is to manage and utilize the implemented system.

The system-operation life cycle includes the daily operations, system maintenance, system enhancements, and system upgrades.

From a Modified Leader's Pen

The transition-implementation process, because of the wide range of different characteristics, requires high levels of focus and the ability to convert from one set of conditions to another. This transition requires exceptional skills from the following stakeholders:

> *Senior management*
> *Business -process owner*
> *End users*
> *System -implementation manager*
> *Functional and technical consultants*
> *Key users*

Senior Management

The role of senior management during the transition-implementation process is to support development through the management of business resources. Successful short-duration global implementations require from senior management:

Commitment
Charisma

Commitment. Strong and decisive leadership is required to open doors when there are factors (such as regional and corporate politics) working against a successful transition.

Charisma. Multicompany and multisystem changes during a big-bang rollout require senior management to show charisma. Senior management has to be alongside of both the end users and the project team to make them feel good and supported.

Business-Process Owner

During the transition-implementation process, the business-process owner must ensure that the agreed-upon process is correctly implemented. As in previous phases, the business-process owner has to show:

Commitment
Courage

Commitment. The business-process owner is responsible for opening doors for the training and resources to ensure the change-management process works.

Courage. The courage to act when things are not going right is essential for the business-process owner. This may mean taking drastic steps, such as dealing with individuals when they are not interested in accepting the new system and are putting the successful execution of a specific business process in danger. While I am on this topic, I believe it is very important to remember that all system-implementation integrators deal with a high-class product and have an obligation when implementing the specific information system to show respect and be successful.

End Users

End users are one of the most critical resources during the transition-implementation process, specifically in system implementations that include multiple countries, sites, and time zones, which make training and change management very difficult and costly. Exceptional leadership qualities are required from the end-user community in the following areas:

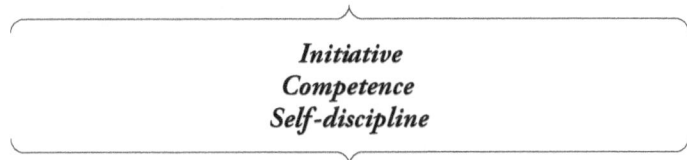

Initiative
Competence
Self-discipline

Initiative. For a successful transition, end users have to show initiative to start using the system to test it out.

Competence. End users show competence by improving their skills and reducing the number of errors that put the quality of the system in danger.

Self-discipline. The end-user community must show self-discipline to challenge all excuses about why the new system is more difficult or different from the old system.

System-Implementation Manager

The system-implementation manager is instrumental in transitioning from the old to the new. In planning and executing the transition, the system-implementation manager has to show the following leadership qualities:

Listening
Courage

Listening. The manager needs to listen to both the project-team members and the end-user community to understand their issues, happiness, and unhappiness.

Courage. Not only is it important to understand, but also to show the courage to act in the long-term interest and stability of the system by correcting and solving issues that arise.

Functional and Technical Consultants

As the functional and technical consultants were responsible for the system configuration and will only be involved with support for a very short period of time after the system goes live, they are expected to show leadership qualities in the following areas:

Judgment
Problem solving

Judgment. The judgment of the functional and technical consultants should be obvious through their enhanced problem-solving capabilities as they get to the root of the problem and solve it.

Problem solving. Instead of trying to solve multiple problems at a time, the consultants are required to solve one problem at a time, bringing stability to the system and comfort to the end users.

Key Users

During the transitioning stage of the system implementation and the system-operation life cycle, the key users are becoming the most knowledgeable permanent source in terms of know-how and understanding. The organization will increasingly depend on their leadership, and as they transition back to their home base, the following qualities are required of them:

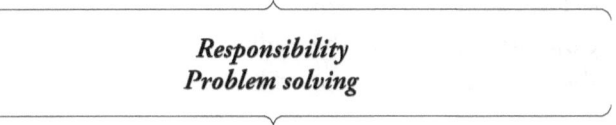

Responsibility Problem solving

Responsibility. The key users are now responsible for getting the job done in terms of training, change management, and support of the end-user community.

Problem solving. Being distributed and away from functional and technical consultants can be overwhelming, and key users' problem-solving leadership qualities will be tested. They have to make sure they tackle the issues one at a time to get the problems solved.

Assessing Your Project-Management Quotient

Based on the definition of the third system-implementation focus area (project transition), the identified roles and responsibilities, and the assigned leadership qualities, I provide below a list of questions or phrases that can be used during the identification, selection, and placement of team members.

Senior Management

Spend time with the potential or proposed senior manager and determine if the person possesses the following leadership qualities:

- **Commitment.** Understand how they make their plans public and follow through with them.
- **Charisma.** Determine to what extent they focus on the project and project-team members rather than themselves.

Business-Process Owner

Spend time with the potential or proposed business-process owner and determine if the person possesses the following leadership qualities:

- **Commitment**. Understand how they make their plans public and follow through with them.
- **Courage.** Ask what the individual has done lately to stretch abilities in a way that caused him or her to feel afraid.

End Users

Spend time with the potential or proposed end user and determine if the person possesses the following leadership qualities:

- **Initiative.** Determine to what extent they are turning opportunities into a final workable product.
- **Competence.** Observe how they reevaluate standards to ensure consistent performance at high levels.
- **Self-discipline**. Seek out any reasons (excuses) they have for not following through with priorities.

System-Implementation Manager

Spend time with the potential or proposed system-implementation manager and determine if the person possesses the following leadership qualities:

Information System Implementations: Using a Leadership Quality Matrix for Success

- **Listening.** Determine if and to what extent the individual schedules time to listen to followers, customers, and competitors.
- **Courage.** Ask what the individual has done lately to stretch abilities in a way that caused him or her to feel afraid.

Functional and Technical Consultants

Spend time with the potential or proposed functional and technical consultants and determine if each person possesses the following leadership qualities:

- **Judgment.** Find out what problems were solved, what the root cause was, and who were the subsequent enablers for proceeding.
- **Problem solving.** Make sure they know of and understand the process of problem solving.

Key Users

Spend time with the potential or proposed key user and determine if the person possesses the following leadership qualities:

- **Responsibility.** Ask what they are doing to achieve excellence.
- **Problem solving.** Make sure they know of and understand the process of problem solving.

Paying attention to material outlined by the Modified Leader's Pen and the Project-Management Quotient sections will allow the system-implementation manager and recruitment specialists to:

- Select the appropriate stakeholders to perform the roles and responsibilities for the project transition focus area of the system implementation.
- Know the leadership qualities for each of the identified roles.
- Ask the right questions to determine if the potential team members possess the required leadership qualities.

Chapter seven will focus on turning the cube to align for the benefit-realization focus area the correct roles and responsibilities and link to those the required leadership qualities.

Chapter Seven

Benefit Realization

Topic Introduction

The fourth implementation-process focus area that requires our attention is benefit realization. All system implementations are done with a specific purpose in mind, and achieving this goal benefits a high percentage of the organization. The benefits for performing the system implementation are expressed in the organization's business plan in the form of business drivers. The business drivers are the core reason for the company's existence and form the basis for the metrics used to compare and validate business performance. In general, business drivers fall into one of three categories: improved performance, increased profitability and/or increased revenue, and earnings growth. A fourth driver, which is not a business driver but rather a project-specific driver, is avoidance of risk due to obsolete computer systems.

It's very important to note that the benefits that form part of the business drivers for implementing the system are not going to just happen during the operational-system life cycle. It takes leadership to drive and realize them. Furthermore, with the project team offsite, the organization structure will be responsible for this realization of the set benefits.

Looking at the traditional system-implementation road map, the benefit-realization process focus area is happening simultaneously with the transitioning-process focus area, which is between the final preparation and the go-live and support phases. The go-live and support phases of the traditional system implementation are intended to move the product from a preproduction environment to a live-production operation.

A failure to realize business benefits at this time indicates that the implementation process was unsuccessful and one of the following focus areas was executed incorrectly: project management, process standardization, transitioning, or troubleshooting.

From a Modified Leader's Pen

As the business benefits were set by the organizational team during the write-up of the business case and the project-management focus area of the implementation process, realizing the benefits requires the attention and focus of the following stakeholders:

$$\left\{ \begin{array}{c} \textit{Business management} \\ \textit{Business -functional experts} \\ \textit{Executive sponsor} \\ \textit{Key and end users} \end{array} \right\}$$

Business Management

Business management is the one group that holds the key to success or failure. Success will allow the business to realize the benefits, while failure will prevent the business system from functioning properly and may even cause it to be eliminated at the end. Business managers are required to exhibit the following leadership qualities:

Initiative. It is the initiative skills of the business-management team that will drive them and end users to optimally use the system to ensure benefit realization.

Security. The business-management team has to provide security to its best people and eliminate those whose unwillingness to change prevents the business from realizing the set benefits.

Business-Functional Experts

During the benefit-realization focus area of the implementation, the business-functional experts are expected to show the following leadership qualities:

Judgment
Passion

Judgment. Through accredited judgment, the business-functional experts will find opportunities to apply the system in ways that will allow for and ensure benefit realization.

Passion. Passionate experts will find methods and approaches to ensure that the implemented system does what it is supposed to do and realizes the set business benefits.

Executive Sponsor

As the senior management team member, the executive sponsor provided the approval and support for the system implementation and has to show the following leadership qualities during the benefit-realization stage:

Responsibility
Vision
Focus

Responsibility. The responsibility to realize the benefits lies with the project sponsor, and it is his or her drive to excellence that will ensure realization of the set benefits.

Vision. Keeping the system-implementation vision in sight helps the sponsor meet the requirements and objectives.

Focus. The project sponsor has to apply the 80/20 rule and stay focused on the 80 percent strengths of the system and not be intimidated by the things that go wrong.

Key and End Users

The key and end users are the only system-implementation team members who, on a day-to-day basis, are performing their work by using the implemented system. The business expects them to show the following leadership qualities:

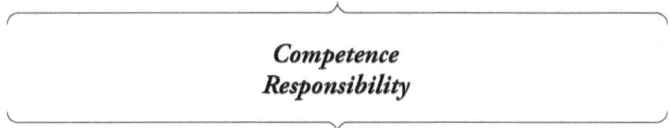

Competence. Following through with transaction execution is a role of the end-user community and is critical to ensure benefit realization.

Responsibility. Taking up the responsibility and going the extra mile to ensure timely transaction execution and data accuracy will allow for realizing global business benefits.

Assessing Your Project-Management Quotient

Based on the definition of the fourth system-implementation focus area (benefit realization), the identified roles and responsibilities, and the assigned leadership qualities, I provide below a list of questions or phrases that can be used during the identification, selection, and placement of team members.

Business Management

Spend time with the potential or proposed business manager and determine if the person possesses the following leadership qualities:

- **Initiative.** Determine if they are risk takers—and if not, find out what scares them about taking risks and their ability to see an opportunity.
- **Security.** Understand what they are doing to give praise (acknowledging contributions) rather than take it.
- **Business-Functional Experts**

Spend time with the potential or proposed business-functional expert and determine if the person possesses the following leadership qualities:

- **Judgment.** Find out when they last acted on a gut feeling and what they learned from the experience.
- **Passion.** Determine whether they spend time with passionate people who can infect them with enthusiasm.

Executive Sponsor

Spend time with the potential or proposed executive sponsor and determine if the person possesses the following leadership qualities:

- **Responsibility.** Understand what the individual is doing to achieve excellence.
- **Vision.** Determine if the individual has a vision and how successful he or she has been in achieving it.
- **Focus.** Find out what the individual's strengths are and the amount of time spent on doing those things.

Key and End Users

Spend time with the potential or proposed key or end user and determine if the person possesses the following leadership qualities:

- **Competence.** Determine if they've felt detached from work, the reasons they have become detached, and plans they put in place to rededicate themselves to work.
- **Responsibility.** Find out what they are doing to equip themselves to become better at what they are doing.

Paying attention to material outlined by the Modified Leader's Pen and the Project-Management Quotient sections will allow the system-implementation manager and recruitment specialists to:

- Select the appropriate stakeholders to perform the roles and responsibilities for the benefit-realization focus area of the system implementation.
- Know the leadership qualities for each of the identified roles.
- Ask the right questions to determine if the potential team members possess the required leadership qualities.

Chapter eight will focus on turning the cube to align for the troubleshooting focus area the correct roles and responsibilities and link to those the required leadership qualities.

Chapter Eight

Troubleshooting

Topic Introduction

Even after careful implementation of the previous four steps—overall project management, standardization, transition, and benefit realization—there will still be issues to resolve. The fifth and final implementation-process focus area that requires our attention is troubleshooting—setting up and maintaining a support organization for end users, not just for the first critical days of your production operation but for long-term support.

The support organization forms the basis for the troubleshooting focus area of the system-implementation process. Throughout the system-operation life cycle, end users will have many questions requiring a solid end-user support organization that is easily accessible by all end users. The support organization is also used to monitor and perform system health checks on a regular basis, and together with key users and functional experts, find opportunities to optimize overall system performance. Having the troubleshooting capability in place completes the system-implementation process and also signals the completion of the project.

Already during the business-process standardization, the organization has to start developing a methodology for troubleshooting the system as a whole. Troubleshooting the business system at all levels requires solid detective skills. When a problem occurs, the list of potential causes is long. The support organization that is leading the troubleshooting effort collects detailed information and systematically narrows the list of potential causes to determine the root problem. This does not provide step-by-step instructions for resolving problems that occur during system implementation. Instead, it describes sound methods for troubleshooting the system by gathering information on the problem, isolating points of failure, and applying techniques to determine the problem's root cause.

The support organization must have the know-how and means to collect sufficient information from users to allow them to isolate the problem. Detailed, accurate information will make this task easier. A form with the correct leading questions will encourage users to provide more details about the problem and also put them into the habit of looking for particular error messages and indicators. Capturing the information electronically will also permit you to retrieve and reexamine it in the future, should the problem repeat itself.

Before focusing on the particular module or systems area where the problem occurred, it might be useful to determine if any configuration or setup changes have been made that might cause the problem. It is recommended that support teams track changes to the lowest level.

After the support team has eliminated obvious problems, they can start applying the many diagnostic techniques to identify problems. The procedures in troubleshooting daily operations specify when to use each tool and provide links to the troubleshooting instructions where appropriate.

From a Modified Leader's Pen

Troubleshooting during the system-operations life cycle requires leadership from both the user community and the organization that was put in place to support the total system environment.

The support organization for the operational environment should be set well in advance of the go-live decision. As support request calls can cover a wide range of areas, such as transaction execution, system enhancements, and reports, an organization consisting of the following is required to ensure in-time resolution:

$$\left\{ \begin{array}{c} \textit{Business -functional experts} \\ \textit{End users} \\ \textit{Key users} \\ \textit{Service and support teams} \end{array} \right\}$$

Business-Functional Experts

On a continual basis, business-functional experts need to evaluate the system to ensure maximum business impact. When performing this action, they are expected to show the following leadership qualities:

Courage
Judgment

Courage. The experts show courage in supporting end users by creating an environment where it is possible for users to have a positive attitude and seek skills improvement.

Judgment. The functional experts are on a higher level than transactional troubleshooting and should be focused on evaluating problems for improvement.

End Users

Although troubleshooting sounds as if it is only the task of the support team, it requires an end-user community with the following leadership qualities:

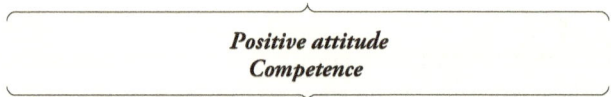

Positive attitude
Competence

Positive attitude. A positive attitude inspires users to improve their level of understanding the system.

Competence. The end users should be able to do troubleshooting themselves and reduce the support-dependent hours to the company.

Key Users

In the case of a global environment, with the key users widely distributed, exceptional leadership qualities are required in the areas of:

Communication
Responsibility

Communication. Very high levels of communication are required from the key users in making sure they convey information in a way that the support organization can use to solve the problem.

Responsibility. The key user's level of responsibility in terms of staying focused on delivering problem-solving results is very important.

Service and Support Teams

Having mastered the skills of problem solving, the support organization must realize that its function is to serve a global user community and express the following leadership qualities:

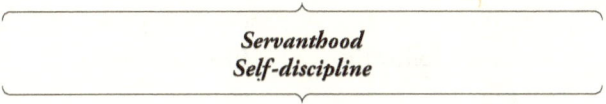

Servanthood
Self-discipline

Servanthood. In serving the end-user community, the teams must stay focused on delivering results on a continual basis.

Self-discipline. The leadership skills required are not on technical problem solving but rather the manner in which it gets done.

Assessing Your Project-Management Quotient

Based on the definition of the fifth system-implementation focus area (troubleshooting), the identified roles and responsibilities, and the assigned leadership qualities, I provide below a list of questions or phrases that can be used during the identification, selection, and placement of team members.

Business-Functional Experts

Spend time with the potential or proposed business-functional expert and determine if the person possesses the following leadership qualities:

- **Courage.** Understand what they are doing to reevaluate standards and ensure consistent performance at high levels.
- **Judgment.** Determine the last time they followed their gut and what was learned from the experience.

End Users

Spend time with the potential or proposed end user and determine if the person possesses the following leadership qualities:

- **Positive attitude.** Find out if potential end users have a pattern of positive achievement.
- **Competence.** Determine what they are doing to keep improving and what time and money are spent to follow through.

Key Users

Spend time with the potential or proposed key user and determine if the person possesses the following leadership qualities:

- **Communication.** Meet with non-defensive mentors to understand whether team members are doing what they communicate.
- **Responsibility.** Determine what they are doing to achieve excellence.

Service and Support Teams

Spend time with the potential or proposed service or support team member and determine if the person possesses the following leadership qualities:

- **Servanthood**. Ask when they last performed acts of kindness for others.
- **Self-discipline**. Determine what method teams are using to set and stay focused on priorities.

Paying attention to material outlined by the Modified Leader's Pen and the Project-Management Quotient sections will allow the system-implementation manager and recruitment specialists to:

- Select the appropriate stakeholders to perform the roles and responsibilities for the troubleshooting focus area of the system implementation.
- Know the leadership qualities for each of the identified roles.
- Ask the right questions to determine if the potential team members possess the required leadership qualities.

This marks the end of the trip—"the trip" referring to the leadership quality matrix. In chapters four to eight I have turned the cube in different directions to align for each implementation process focus area the correct roles and responsibilities and link to those the required leadership qualities. As indicated, this as a matter of fact is the leadership quality matrix. The table in Appendix B of this book provides the leadership quality matrix in a tabular format.

In section three I focus on the instruments available to prepare for the trip. This section focuses on the various leadership models that are available to assist recruitment specialists to determine if potential team members have the leadership qualities as defined by the leadership quality matrix.

Section Three

Diagnostic Instruments

Chapter Nine

Selection of Diagnostic Instruments

Topic Introduction

In the first section of this book, the focus was on defining the various key stakeholders and their roles and responsibilities; in the second section, the focus was on putting together the leadership quality matrix—namely, the definition of the implementation process. During the definition of the implementation process, the focus was on determining the leadership qualities required. In this section, the focus is on the diagnostic instruments available to assist the staffing team in selecting team members with the required leadership qualities.

To refresh your memory, below is a summary of leadership qualities for each implementation-process focus area. The identified leadership qualities form the basis for identifying the diagnostic instruments to assess whether the various team members have the leadership qualities required to successfully complete the system implementation.

As mentioned in chapter two of this book, the success of any information-system implementation equally depends on both the organization and the implementation team, with this in mind I am using the opportunity to also summarize the leadership qualities requirements for the organizational team and the project team.

Project Management

Diagnostic instruments are required to assess:

- The project team's servanthood, competence, communication, character, commitment, passion, courage, judgment, problem solving, self-discipline, and responsibility.
- The organization team's commitment and vision.

Process Standardization

Diagnostic instruments are required to assess:

- The project team's responsibility, competence, and judgment.
- The organization team's character, commitment, courage, vision, initiative, and problem solving.

Transition

Diagnostic instruments are required to assess:

- The project team's courage, listening, judgment, problem solving, and responsibility.
- The organization team's charisma, commitment, courage, competence, initiative, and self-discipline.

Business Realization

Diagnostic instruments are required to assess:

- The project team's responsibility and competence.
- The organization team's initiative, security, judgment, passion, competence, responsibility, vision, and focus.

Troubleshooting

Diagnostic instruments are required to assess:

- The project team's communication, responsibility, servanthood, and self-discipline.
- The organization team's courage, judgment, competence, positive attitude, communication, and responsibility.

Diagnostic Instruments

Though I've tried numerous diagnostic assessment instruments in my twenty-four years of experience, I have found the following options to be the most relevant, applicable, and easy to use.

> *Personality grid*
> *Group-development process*
> *Decision-authority leadership model*
> *Superior-subordinate power-relationship model*
> *Supportive vs. directive behavior leadership model*
> *Leadership vs. management matrix*
> *Strategic side vs. personal sides of leadership model*

This overview is not intended to educate system-implementation recruitment and placement teams on how to use the various instruments, just to create awareness of when the individual diagnostic assessment instruments can be used, what they are focused on, and how they work.

Personality Grid

The Merrill-Reid personality analysis as described by Peter Urs Bender (1997:60–66) is useful for allowing individuals to understand themselves and their fellow team members better. After team members consider their own personality type, they share and compare with the other members. There is no right or wrong personality type. Each of the personality types has its own needs, values, and motivations, as well as different levels of assertiveness and responsiveness. (More information on the Merrill-Reid personality analysis can be found in a publication titled *Personal Styles and Effective Performance* by David W. Merrill and Roger H. Reid, 1991.)

The Merrill-Reid personality grid, as shown by the figure below, groups personality types as analytical, driven, expressive, and amiable.

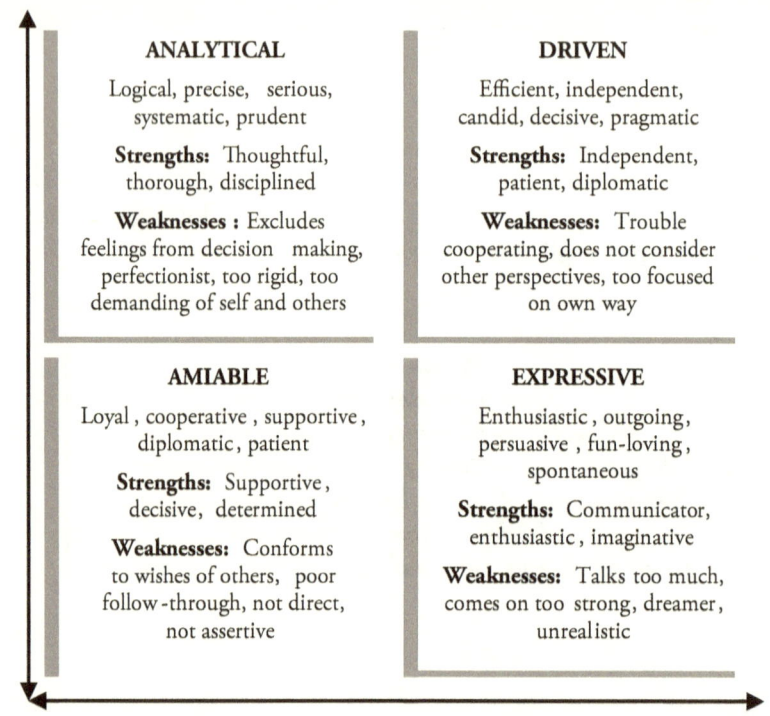

Figure 9.1: Merrill-Reid Personality Grid
(Derived from Urs-Bender, 1997)

Group-Development Process

The Tuckman-Jensen group-development diagnostic tool as described by Pinto and Millet (1999:124) is helpful in assessing the molding of an effective implementation team with a strong focus on a dynamic group-development process. The group-development assessment tool assists in determining where the team is in terms of maturity. This holds true for groups formed across different organizations and for different purposes.

The Tuckman-Jensen group-development process, as shown by the figure below, consists of the following five stages: forming, storming, norming, performing, and adjourning. (More information on the

Tuckman-Jensen group-development diagnostic tool can be found in a publication titled *Stages in Small Group Development Revisited: Group and Organizational Studies* by B. W. Tuchman and M. A. Jensen, 1977.)

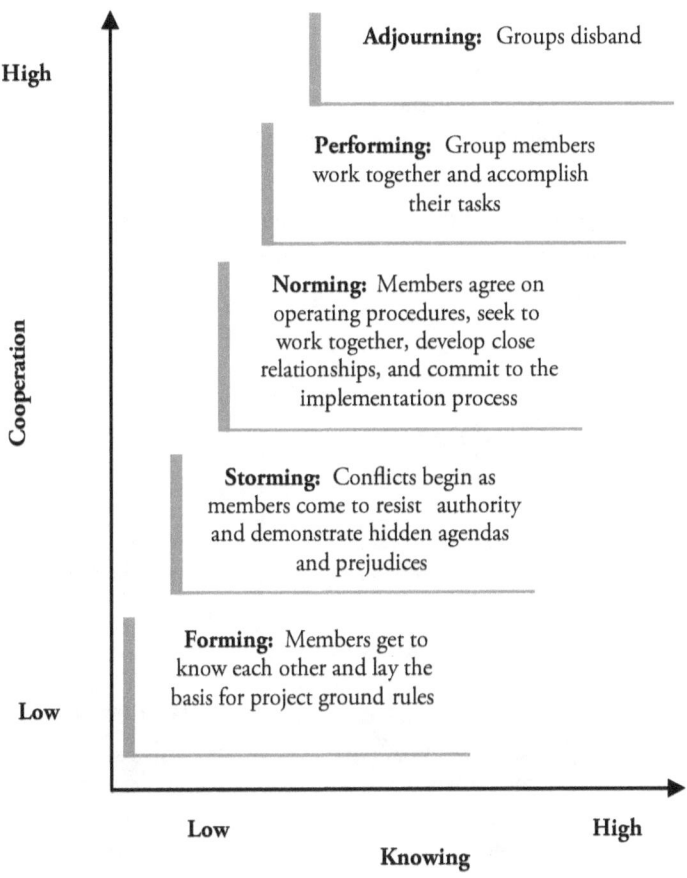

Figure 9.2: Tuckman-Jensen Group-Development Process
(Derived from Pinto and Millet, 1999)

Decision-Authority Leadership Model

With regard to decision making, Pinto and Millet (1999:140), based on the Bonoma-Slevin leadership model, outline that each and every decision consists of the following two dimensions and both have to be answered prior to making the decision: (1) from where and from whom the information input will come, and (2) where the decision-making authority resides or who makes the decision.

According to Pinto and Millet, both dimensions are critical for effective leadership. In order to ensure that decisions get made on time, it is important for the system-implementation manager to understand where information will come from and who will be making the decisions. Furthermore, the system-implementation manager should know whether the decision makers will be making decisions on a group or individual basis and with a high or low volume of input.

The Bonoma-Slevin leadership model, as shown by the figure below, categorizes leaders in the following four styles: consensus, consultative, autocrat, and shareholder.

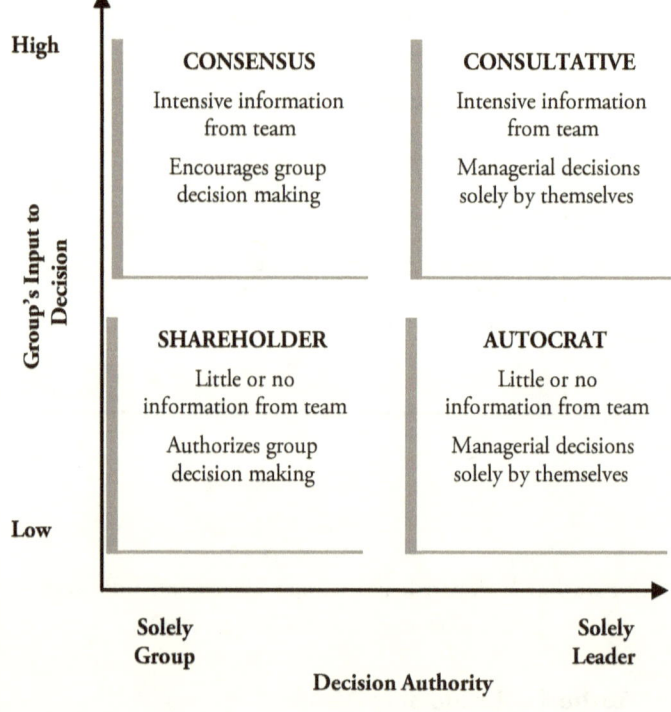

Figure 9.3: Bonoma-Slevin Leadership Model
(Derived from Pinto and Millet, 1999)

Superior-Subordinate Power-Relationship Model

The Kets de Vries (2001:217) superior-subordinate power-relationship model is a helpful tool to assess the "follower" characteristics of various project-team members. Follower assessment is important to determine the mind-set of the various project-team members, their expectations, and their "power relationship" with the leader.

Kets de Vries's model, as shown by the figure below, sorts group leaders into the following four categories: strong guidance, balance, self-management through teams, and sense of drifting.

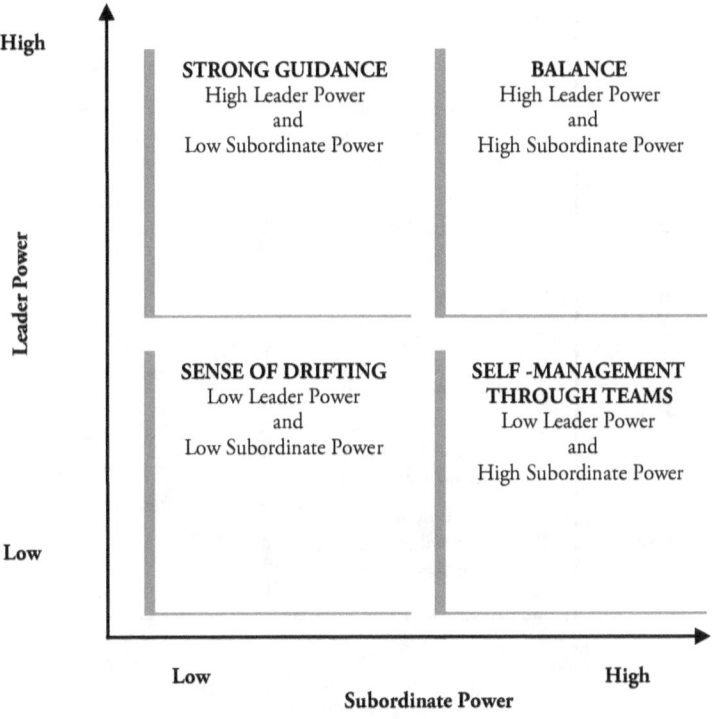

Figure 9.4: Superior-Subordinate Power-Relationship Model
(Derived from Kets de Vries, 2001:217)

Supportive vs. Directive Behavior Leadership Model

According to G. Pansegrouw (1986:68), the more the supervisor can adjust his or her leadership style to fit the task readiness of the workers, the more effective he or she will be in influencing the worker's behavior. Any leadership style can be applicable and correct as long as it correlates with the task readiness of the subordinates.

Pansegrouw's model, as shown by the figure below, sorts leaders into the following categories: supporting style, coaching style, directing style and delegating style.

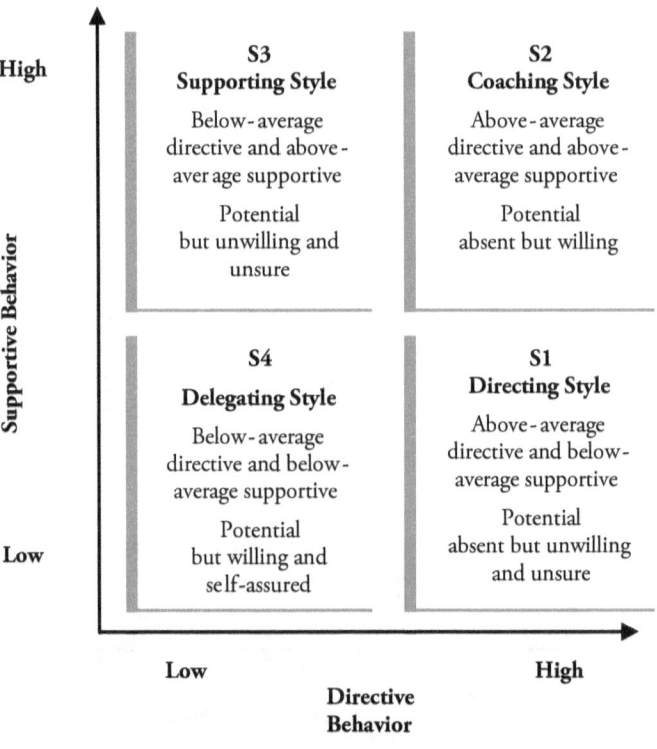

Figure 9.5: Supportive Behavior vs. Directive Behavior Leadership Model (Derived from Pansegrouw, 1986:68)

Leadership vs. Management Matrix

Kets de Vries (2001:253) stresses the importance of differentiating between leaders and managers. Leaders are people doing the right things, while managers are people doing things right. Leaders can be described as people who are interested in the future, interested in change, long-term oriented, and caught up in vision. They know how to deal with why's, empower people, simplify, and use intuition, and they have a wider view that encompasses social concerns.

Managers are people who focus on the present, prefer stability, focus on the short term, focus on instructions, deal with how's, tend to control, rely on logic, and are more preoccupied by corporate concern.

Kets de Vries's model, as shown by the figure below, sorts leaders into four categories: visionaries, stars, busy bees and drifters.

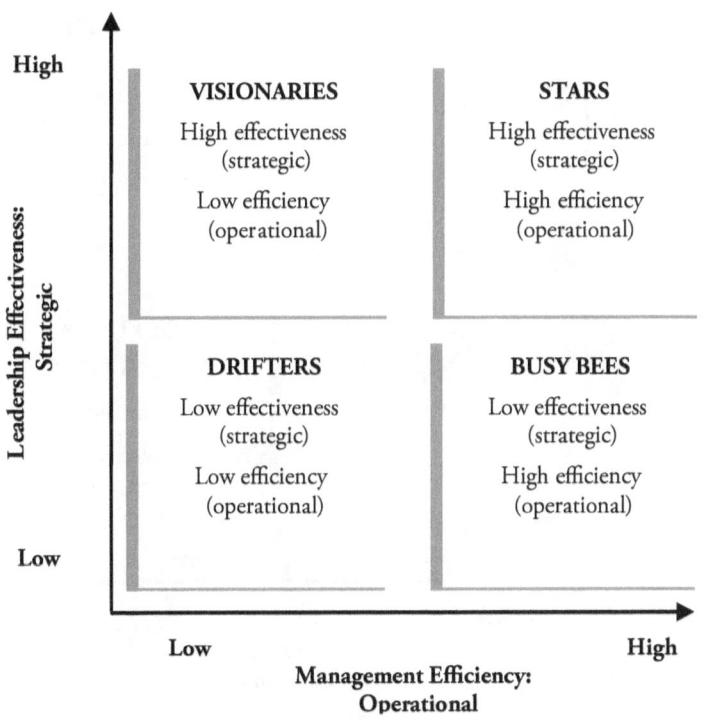

Figure 9.6: Leadership vs. Management Matrix
(Derived from Kets de Vries, 2001:253)

Strategic Side vs. Personal Sides of Leadership Model

According to Peter Koestenbaum (2002:52), the strategic side of leadership as usually conceived is not enough. It is on the personal side of leadership (in the sense of greatness, focusing on people, their souls and hearts, their meaning and destination) that the next breakthrough in business will occur.

As quoted by Koestenbaum (2002:55), Napoleon said that "the art of choosing is not nearly as difficult as the art of enabling those one has chosen to attain their full worth."

Koestenbaum's model, as shown by the figure below, sorts leaders in the following four categories: distinction, opportunities, death, and cynicism.

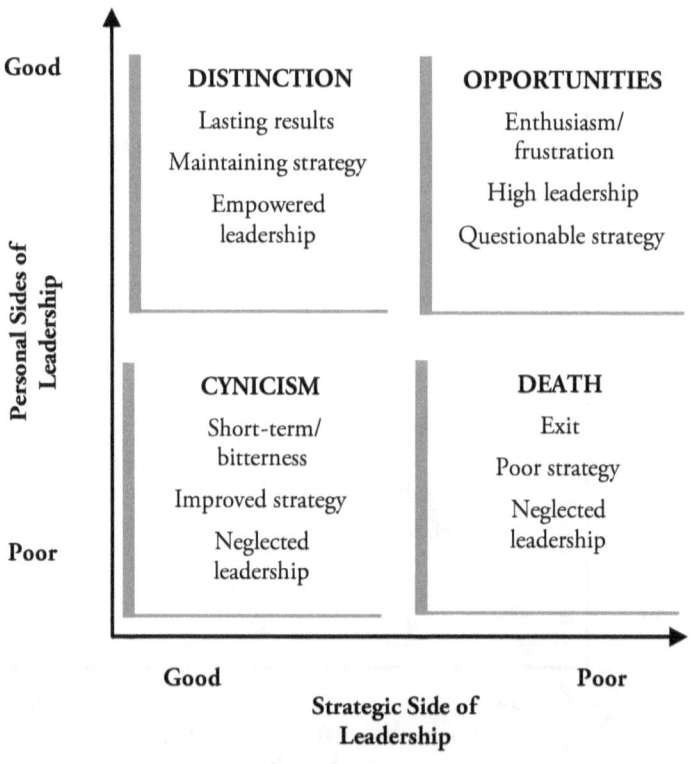

Figure 9.7: Strategic Side vs. Personal Sides of Leadership Model (Derived from Koestenbaum, 2002:)

From a Modified Leader's Pen

The character of the system-implementation manager will determine whether he or she can rally all team members to complete short-duration system-implementation projects. In order to do this, it is important that the system-implementation manager, as in any other team event, select the correct combinations to bring together the team that will suit the specific system-implementation dynamics.

The diagnostic instruments described above are important focus areas of the system-implementation manager's tool kit. The diagnostic instruments are used to support the leadership quality matrix. They help identify to what extent various team members have the leadership qualities required of them in their specific roles.

In my national and international projects, I have used all of the following diagnostic instruments with a great deal of success:

> *Personality grid*
> *Group-development process*
> *Decision-authority leadership model*
> *Superior-subordinate power-relationship model*
> *Supportive vs. directive behavior leadership model*
> *Leadership vs. management matrix*
> *Strategic side vs. personal sides of leadership model*

Personality Grid

The personality-grid model helps the system-implementation manager identify team members who have the needed leadership qualities of communication, problem solving, and positive attitude.

> *Communication*
> *Problem solving*
> *Positive attitude*

Group-Development Process

The group-development process helps the system-implementation manager identify team members who are working as a synchronized unit to deliver the system implementation focusing on the project overall.

Project overall

Decision-Authority Leadership Model

The decision-authority leadership model helps the system-implementation manager identify team members who have the specific leadership qualities of judgment when required.

Judgment

Superior-Subordinate Power-Relationship Model

The superior-subordinate power-relationship model helps the system-implementation manager identify team members who have specific leadership qualities of competence and courage when required.

Competence
Courage

Supportive vs. Directive Behavior Leadership Model

The supportive versus directive behavior leadership model helps the system-implementation manager identify team members who have specific leadership qualities of responsibility and listening when required.

Responsibility
Listening

Leadership vs. Management Matrix

The leadership versus management matrix helps the system-implementation manager identify team members who have specific leadership qualities of vision, passion, self-discipline, and servanthood when required.

Vision
Passion
Self-discipline
Servanthood

Strategic Side vs. Personal Sides of Leadership Model

The strategic side versus personal sides of leadership model helps the system-implementation manager identify team members who have specific leadership qualities of character, commitment, charisma, initiative, and security when required.

Character
Commitment
Charisma
Initiative
Security

Assessing Your Project-Management Quotient

Based on the diagnostic instruments that have been identified to assist in determining the various leadership qualities, I provide below a checklist that can be used during the identification, selection, and placement of team members.

When selecting project or organization team members, use the following instruments to determine if the candidates have the correct leadership qualities:

- **Personality grid.** Use this instrument to help individuals understand themselves and other team members better.
- **Group-development process.** After assessing the leader and the task to be performed, this instrument also assesses the follower.
- **Decision-authority leadership model.** Use this to discover whether the decision makers will be making decisions based on group or individual input, at high or low volume.
- **Superior-subordinate power relationship model** and **supportive vs. directive behavior leadership model.** These instruments both determine whether the leadership style correlates with the task readiness of the subordinates.
- **Leadership vs. management matrix.** Ensure that the system-implementation manager understands the team and the team is aware of the system-implementation manager's leadership effectiveness.
- **Strategic side vs. personal sides of leadership model.** Determine where the leadership focus of the project lies: project sponsor, senior management, or business-process owner.

Though I earlier indicated that this is an overview and my intention is not to educate system-implementation recruitment and placement teams on how to use the various instruments but rather to create awareness of when the individual diagnostic assessment instruments can be used, what they are focused on, and how they work, let me help.

I can hear the comments: *This is too complicated! This is too much work! This is not working in practice!* Let me explain. Appendix C provides a complete description of which diagnostic instruments should be used to determine whether potential candidates possess the required leadership qualities; I am not going to repeat it. I will rather focus on an interpretive example.

I have not touched on this, though I believe you would have realized it reading through the leadership quality section (chapters four to eight): a single leadership quality can take different shapes and forms.

Example: For this example we will use the problem-solving leadership quality. During the process-standardization focus area from a problem-solving perspective, the functional experts should have the ability to anticipate problems that can occur because of standardization or a specific design (chapter five). During the troubleshooting focus area with regard to problem solving, key users have to make sure they tackle the issues one at a time to get the problems solved (chapter eight).

As I indicated earlier in this chapter, the Merrill-Reid personality grid can be used to determine if potential candidates have the problem-solving leadership quality. The Merrill-Reid personality grid can place a candidate in any one of four quadrants: analytical, driven, expressive, or amiable.

With regard to the functional expert, it is recommended to choose a candidate in the analytical quadrant, as this person will be logical, precise, serious, systematic, and prudent and have the strength to be thoughtful, thorough, and disciplined.

With regard to the key user, it is recommended to choose a candidate in the driven quadrant, as this person will be efficient, independent, candid, decisive, and pragmatic and have the strengths to be independent, patient, and diplomatic.

To learn more on how to use and apply the various diagnostic instruments, study the material from references outlined in this chapter.

In section three, I have focused on the instruments available to prepare for the trip. This section focused on the various leadership models that are available to assist recruitment specialists to determine if potential team members have the leadership qualities as defined by the leadership quality matrix (chapters four to eight).

Conclusion

Topic Introduction

In conclusion, I want to outline the viewpoints of exceptional and well-published authors like John Maxwell, Oren Harari, Manfred Kets de Vries, Peter Urs Bender, and John the Baptist that have impacted my life and stimulated the modified leadership passion in me.

In the words of John Maxwell, author of *The 21 Indispensable Qualities of a Leader* (1999), as leaders we must remember that "our capacity will be determined by our ability to rally people and that our leadership capabilities will not rise above our own abilities."

Oren Harari, author of *The Leadership Secrets of Colin Powell* (2002), wrote that "leadership is the art of accomplishing more than the science of management says is possible."

As a leadership change agent, I want to express the strength of my feelings about the role of leadership in successful system implementations by quoting the words of Manfred Kets de Vries, author of *The Leadership Mystique* (2001): "Your business can have all the advantages in the world, strong financial resources, enviable market position, and a state-of-the-art technology, but if leadership fails, all of these advantages melt away."

Peter Koestenbaum, author of *Leadership: The Inner Side of Greatness* (2002), wrote about "the Leadership Diamond model . . . a paradigm that challenges every person to transform their thinking and approach everything with fresh effectiveness in order to reap richer results and become a great leader."

Peter Urs Bender, author of *Leadership from Within* (1997), urges you not to wait to become a leader—start now. "To be a leader, feel like a leader, act like a leader, express like a leader, be seen as a leader, follow other leaders, and see and support the leader in others."

Finally, in the book of Mark 10:43–45 (Hayford et al, 1991), John the Baptist is very clear on the only way to become a great leader: "Whoever wants to become great among you must be your servant, and whoever wants to be first must be a slave to all. For even the Son of Man did not come to be served, but to serve."

From a Modified Leader's Pen

Through the insight provided to me by Romans 12:3–8, various other well-published authors, and my experience over the past twenty-four years, I have succeeded in putting together the leadership quality matrix, an instrument that is geared toward providing significant momentum to information-system implementations.

I hope you have enjoyed reading *Information System Implementations: Using a Leadership Quality Matrix for Success.*

I trust and believe you have gained intellectual capital for your knowledge workers, geared toward providing significant momentum to your system implementations.

Appendix A: A Step-by-Step Approach

The figure below provides the system-implementation recruitment and placement teams with a step-by-step approach to what they need to know to staff the system-implementation project with team members that have the required leadership qualities.

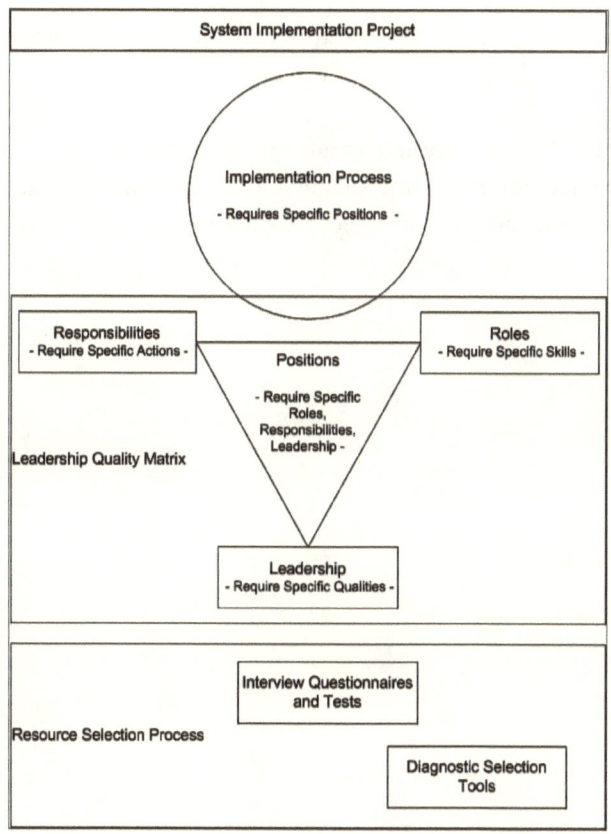

Figure Appendix A.1: A Step-by-Step Approach

Based on the figure above, the following twelve steps can support and guide the system-implementation recruitment and placement teams in staffing the systems implementation project with team members with the required leadership qualities:

- Determine the relevant system-implementation process focus areas.
- Determine the applicable positions.
- Determine for each position the required roles and responsibilities.
- Determine for each role the relevant skills required.
- Determine for each role the required leadership qualities.
- Compile for each role a leadership-quality interview questionnaire.
- Compile for each role the applicable diagnostic instrument list.
- Identify the potential candidates.
- Perform interview.
- Candidate to complete diagnostic instrument(s).
- Evaluate interview and diagnostic instrument outcomes.
- Approve and place or reject candidate.

Appendix B: Leadership Quality Matrix

With regard to the leadership quality matrix, I want to repeat what I have said in the preface:

- This book and its insights are based on my personal experience and mine only.
- Furthermore, this book is not intended to be an exhaustive list of facts; it includes only those that deserve our immediate attention.

It is my real-life experiences since 1996 that have allowed me to develop the leadership quality matrix and my modified leadership style. The cube below demonstrates the three dimensions of the leadership quality matrix.

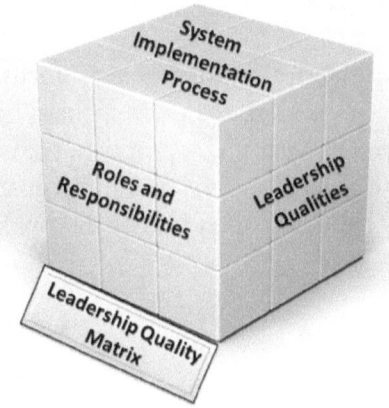

Figure Appendix B.1: Dimensions of Leadership Quality Matrix

The cube demonstrates the fact that though there is a fixed set of stakeholders, implementation processes, and leadership qualities, the requirements will change as the combination where they stand in relation to each other changes.

In the table below, I provide in tabular format the material I have described in chapters four to eight of this book. The table below provides for each of the described roles:

- The system-implementation focus area they are involved in
- The leadership qualities required during the specific system-implementation focus area

I can hear your comment: "So what! How can I use this in practice?" Let me explain. Transfer the information in the table below onto a spreadsheet and use the table as a check sheet throughout the system-implementation project. Using the spreadsheet, the system-implementation manager can evaluate and control the following:

- Whether all the roles for a specific system-implementation focus area have been identified
- Whether the identified role(s) have been filled
- Whether the individual executing the role has the required leadership qualities

Example: During the project-management focus area of the system implementation project, has an executive sponsor been appointed; and if so, does the individual have the appropriate commitment and vision leadership qualities? For details on the commitment and vision leadership qualities, please refer back to chapter four of this book.

Information System Implementations: Using a Leadership Quality Matrix for Success

Role and Responsibility	Chronological Tasks	Required Leadership Quality
All Project Team Members	Project Management	
		Seek fulfillment
		Make progress
		Create results

Role and Responsibility	Chronological Tasks	Required Leadership Quality
Executive Sponsor	Project Management	
		Commitment
		Vision
	Benefit Realization	
		Initiative
		Security
		Responsibility
		Vision
		Focus

Role and Responsibility	Chronological Tasks	Required Leadership Quality
Senior Management	Transition	
		Commitment
		Charisma

Role and Responsibility	Chronological Tasks	Required Leadership Quality
Business-Process Owners	Process Standardization	
		Character
		Commitment
		Courage
		Vision
	Transition	
		Commitment
		Courage

Role and Responsibility	Chronological Tasks	Required Leadership Quality
Business-Functional Experts	Process Standardization	
		Initiative
		Problem solving
	Benefit Realization	
		Judgment
		Passion
	Troubleshooting	
		Courage
		Judgment

Role and Responsibility	Chronological Tasks	Required Leadership Quality
End Users	Transition	
		Initiative
		Competence
		Self-discipline
	Benefit Realization	
		Competence
		Responsibility
	Troubleshooting	
		Positive attitude
		Competence

Information System Implementations: Using a Leadership Quality Matrix for Success

Role and Responsibility	Chronological Tasks	Required Leadership Quality
System-Implementation Manager	Project Management	
		Servanthood
		Competence
		Communication
		Character
		Commitment
		Passion
		Courage
		Judgment
		Problem solving
	Transition	
		Listening
		Courage

Role and Responsibility	Chronological Tasks	Required Leadership Quality
Team Leaders	Project Management	
		Responsibility
		Courage
		Self-discipline
		Judgment
		Problem solving

Role and Responsibility	Chronological Tasks	Required Leadership Quality
Functional and Technical Experts (Consultants)	Process Standardization	
		Responsibility
		Competence
	Transition	
		Judgment
		Problem solving

Role and Responsibility	Chronological Tasks	Required Leadership Quality
Key Users	Process Standardization	
		Judgment
		Responsibility
	Transition	
		Responsibility
		Problem solving
	Benefit Realization	
		Competence
		Responsibility
	Troubleshooting	
		Communication
		Responsibility

Role and Responsibility	Chronological Tasks	Required Leadership Quality
Service and Support Teams	Troubleshooting	
		Servanthood
		Self-discipline

Appendix C: Diagnostic Instruments

With regard to diagnostic instruments as a mechanism to identify various leadership qualities, I want to repeat what I have said in the preface:

- This book and its insights are based on my personal experience and mine only.
- Furthermore, this book is not intended to be an exhaustive list of facts; it includes only those that deserve our immediate attention.

It is my real-life experiences since 1996 that have allowed me to use the outcome of the various diagnostic instruments to identify whether individuals have the required leadership qualities.

In the table below, I provide in tabular format the material that I have described in chapter nine of this book. The table below provides an indication of:

- The relevant diagnostic instruments
- The leadership qualities that can be assessed by completing a specific diagnostic instrument

Once more I can hear the comment, "So what! How can I use this in practice?" Again, let me explain. Transfer the information in the table below onto a spreadsheet and use the table as a check sheet throughout the system implementation project. Using the spreadsheet, the system-implementation manager can determine the specific diagnostic instruments to be used to assess the various leadership qualities.

Example: Based on Appendix B, during the project-management focus area of the system implementation project, an executive sponsor is required, and the individual should have commitment and vision leadership qualities. A potential candidate to fill the project sponsor position has been identified. Based on Appendix C, the recruitment specialist and systems-implementation manager will ask the identified candidate to complete both the leadership vs. management matrix and the strategic side vs. personal sides of leadership model diagnostic instruments. The outcome of the mentioned diagnostic instruments will provide an indication whether the potential candidate has vision and commitment leadership qualities. For details on the leadership vs. management matrix and the strategic side vs. personal sides of leadership model diagnostic instruments, please refer back to chapter nine of this book.

Diagnostic Instruments	Leadership Qualities
Personality Grid	Communication Problem solving Positive attitude
Group-Development Process	Project overall
Decision-Authority Leadership Model	Judgment
Superior-Subordinate Power-Relationship Model	Competence Courage
Supportive vs. Directive Behavior Leadership Model	Responsibility Listening
Leadership vs. Management Matrix	Vision Passion Self-discipline Servanthood
Strategic Side vs. Personal Sides of Leadership Model	Character Commitment Charisma Initiative Security

References

Galorath, Dan. June 7, 2008. *Better Estimation & Planning Can Help: Software Project Failure Costs Billions.* (http://www.galorath.com/wp/software-project-failure-costs-billions-better-estimation-planning-can-help.php)

Harari, Oren. 2002. *The Leadership Secrets of Colin Powell.* New York: McGraw-Hill.

Hayford, J. W., S. Middlebrook, J. Horner, and M. A. Matsdorf. 1991. *Spirit Filled Life Bible: New King James Version.* Nashville: Thomas Nelson, Inc.

Kalyan City Life Blog. August 30, 2011. *Five Bases of Power by John French and Bertram H. Raven.* (http://kalyan-city.blogspot.com/2011/08/five-bases-of-power-by-john-french-and.html)

Kets de Vries, Manfred. 2001. *The Leadership Mystique: A User's Manual for the Human Enterprise.* London: Pearson Education Limited.

Koestenbaum, Peter. 2002. *Leadership: The Inner Side of Greatness: A Philosophy for Leaders.* San Francisco: John Wiley & Sons Inc.

Krigsman, Michael. January 10, 2008. *New research: IT cost overruns, delays and contract terminations.* (http://www.zdnet.com/blog/projectfailures/new-research-it-cost-overruns-delays-and-contract-terminations/565)

Krigsman, Michael. March 1, 2011. *2011 ERP survey: New IT failure research and statistics.* (http://www.zdnet.com/blog/projectfailures/2011-erp-survey-new-it-failure-research-and-statistics/12486)

Maxwell, C. John. 1999. *The 21 Indispensable Qualities of a Leader: Becoming the Person Others Will Follow.* Nashville: Thomas Nelson, Inc.

Merrill, David W., and Roger H. Reid. 1991. *Personal Styles and Effective Performance: Make Your Style Work For You.* Boca Raton, Florida: CRC Press LLC.

Pansegrouw, G. 1986. *Leadership Strategies for Organizational Transformation.* 7th Edition. Englewood Cliffs, New Jersey: Prentice Hall.

Pinto, K. Jeffrey, and Ido Millet. 1999. *Successful Information System Implementation: The Human Side.* Newton Square, PA: Project Management Institute, Inc.

Tuchman, B.W, and Jensen, M.A. 1977. *Stages in Small Group Development Revisited: Group and Organizational Studies;* 2, 419-427.

Urs Bender, Peter. 1997. *Leadership from Within.* Toronto: Stoddart Publishing Co. Limited.

Recommended Reading

Covey, Stephen R. 1992. *Principle-Centered Leadership*. New York: Simon & Schuster, Inc.

International Bible Society. 1998. *The Holy Bible: New International Version (Electronic Edition)*. Nashville: Parsons Technology, Inc.

Jones, Laurie Beth. 1995. *Jesus CEO: Using Ancient Wisdom for Visionary Leadership*. New York: Hyperion.

Julian, Larry. 2002. *God Is My CEO: Following God's Principles in a Bottom-Line World*. Avon, MA: Adams Media Corporation.

Krames, Jeffrey A. 2003. *What the Best CEOs Know: 7 Exceptional Leaders and Their Lessons for Transforming Any Business*. New York: McGraw-Hill.

Lencioni, Patrick. 2002. *The Five Dysfunctions of a Team: A Leadership Fable*. San Francisco: Jossey-Bass.

MacArthur, John F. 1997. *The Power of Integrity: Building a Life Without Compromise*. Wheaton, Illinois: Crossway Books.

Strobel, Lee. 1998. *The Case for Christ: A Journalist's Personal Investigation of the Evidence for Jesus*. Grand Rapids, MI: Zondervan.

Swindoll, Charles. 2007. *Hand Me Another Brick: How Effective Leaders Motivate Themselves and Others*. Nashville: Word Publishing Group.

Yaverbaum, Eric. 2004. *Leadership Secrets of the World's Most Successful CEOs: 100 Top Executives Reveal the Management Strategies that Made Their Companies Great*. Chicago: Dearborn Trade Publishing.

Index

Benefit realization, 28, 53, 54, 55, 56, 57, 59, 60, 91, 92, 94
Business-functional expert, 15, 16, 42, 43, 56, 58, 62, 63, 92
Business-process owner, 14, 18, 42, 43, 45, 49, 51, 52, 82, 92
Bonoma-Slevin, 73, 74

Character, 15, 21, 35, 39, 43, 45, 48, 70, 75, 79, 81, 92, 93, 96
Charisma, 48, 52, 70, 81, 91, 96
Commitment, 21, 23, 35-40, 43, 45, 48, 49, 52, 70, 81, 90, 91-93, 96
Communication, 8, 16, 19, 27, 28, 33-35, 39, 63, 64, 70, 71, 79, 93, 94, 96
Competence, 35, 39, 44, 46, 49, 50, 52, 57, 58, 62, 64, 70, 71, 80, 92-94
Courage, 35-37, 39, 43-45, 49, 50, 52, 53, 61, 62, 64, 70, 71, 74, 80, 92, 93, 96

Decision-authority leadership model, 73, 80
Diagnostic instruments, 69-71, 79, 81, 82, 95, 96

End user, 6, 13, 14, 16, 48-52, 55, 57, 58, 60, 62, 64, 92

Focus areas, xv, 5, 28, 29, 33, 38, 40, 41, 45-47, 51, 53-57, 59, 60, 63, 65, 69, 79, 83, 88, 90, 95
Functional consultant, 17, 19, 92, 93

Group-development process, 71-73, 79, 80, 82, 96

Initiative, xvi, 6, 18, 43, 45, 49, 50, 52, 55, 58, 70, 81, 91, 92, 96

Judgment, xiv, 35, 37, 39, 44-46, 50, 51, 53, 56, 58, 62, 64, 70, 70, 71, 80, 92-94, 96

Kets de Vries, x, 20, 21, 25, 75, 77
Key users, 42, 44-46, 48, 51, 53, 60-64, 83, 94
Koestenbaum, x, 78, 85, 97

Leadership vs. management matrix, 71, 77, 79, 81, 96
Leadership quality matrix, xiii, xiv, xv, 3, 5, 7, 13, 29, 65, 79, 86, 89

Pansegrouw, 76, 98
Passion, x, 35, 36, 38, 39, 56, 58, 70, 81, 85, 92, 93, 96

Personality grid, 71, 72, 79, 83, 96
Phases, 10, 25, 29, 35, 41, 49, 54
Pinto and Millet, 25-27, 73, 74
Positions, 14, 17, 36, 88
Positive attitude, 62, 64, 79, 92, 96
Problem solving, 35, 37, 40, 43, 50, 51, 53, 63, 70, 79, 83, 90, 93, 94, 96
Process standardization, 41, 43, 60, 70, 92-94
Project management, xvi, 33, 70, 91, 93

Responsibility, xi, 5, 14, 20, 26, 36-39, 44-46, 51, 53, 56-58, 63, 64, 70, 71, 80, 81, 91-94, 96

Security, 55, 58, 70, 81, 91, 96
Self-discipline, 37, 39, 50, 52, 63, 64, 70, 71, 81, 92-94, 96
Senior management, 13, 43, 48, 52, 82, 91
Servanthood, 35, 39, 63, 64, 70, 71, 81, 93, 94, 96
Service and support team, 16, 18, 61, 63, 64, 94
Strategic side vs. personal sides of leadership model, 78, 81, 82, 96
Superior-subordinate power-relationship model, 71, 75, 79, 80
Supportive vs. directive behavior leadership model, 71, 76, 79, 80
System-implementation manager, 6, 17, 18, 20, 21, 35, 36, 39, 40, 46, 48, 50, 52, 53, 59, 64, 74, 79-82, 90, 93

Team leaders, 5, 6, 18, 34, 36, 37, 39, 93
Technical consultants, 19, 42, 44, 46, 48, 50, 51, 53
Transition, 28, 46-55, 60, 70, 91-94
Troubleshooting, 27, 28, 55, 59-63, 65, 70, 83, 92, 94

Vision, 14, 15, 26, 37, 38, 43, 56, 58, 70, 77, 80, 90-92, 96

About the Author

I have had a truly extraordinary career. My tale is of a child of farmers, reflecting discipline, high standards, hard work, and high integrity. Today, I am viewed as a well-respected system-development and system-implementation leader by my colleagues and team members. Over the years, I have dedicated myself to adding value to my employers and team members. I was born on September 25, 1961, in Niekershoop, a very small farming community in Northern Cape Province, South Africa, to Francois and Martha Jacobs, both from the traditional South Africa farming culture.

Since I started my career in 1985, my international system-implementation experience has included work in countries like Brazil, Canada, the Caribbean, Kazakhstan, Russia, South Africa, and the United States. The biggest value I bring to my employer is my understanding of information systems from both operational and consulting perspectives. I have management (general, project, and business-administration), analysis (business-information and business-process), and information (systems and technology) knowledge and experience in the consulting, chemical, metals, manufacturing, and agricultural industries.

My leadership and coaching are driven by my self-motivation, analytical capability, people orientation, and ability to communicate with people in all walks of life.

My knowledge and experience are strengthened by my formal education: PhD, Price Decision Support Systems, May 2000 (North-West University, South Africa); M Com, Financial Information for the Management Process, 1993 (University of South Africa, South Africa); BEcon (Hon), Marketing, Finance, Information, and Control Systems, 1987 (Bloemfontain University, South Africa); and BAgric, Economics, Business, and Agricultural Economics, 1983 (Bloemfontain University, South Africa).

www.ingramcontent.com/pod-product-compliance
Lightning Source LLC
Chambersburg PA
CBHW030840180526
45163CB00004B/1392